A Hundred Glimpses of Paris

Mina Carson

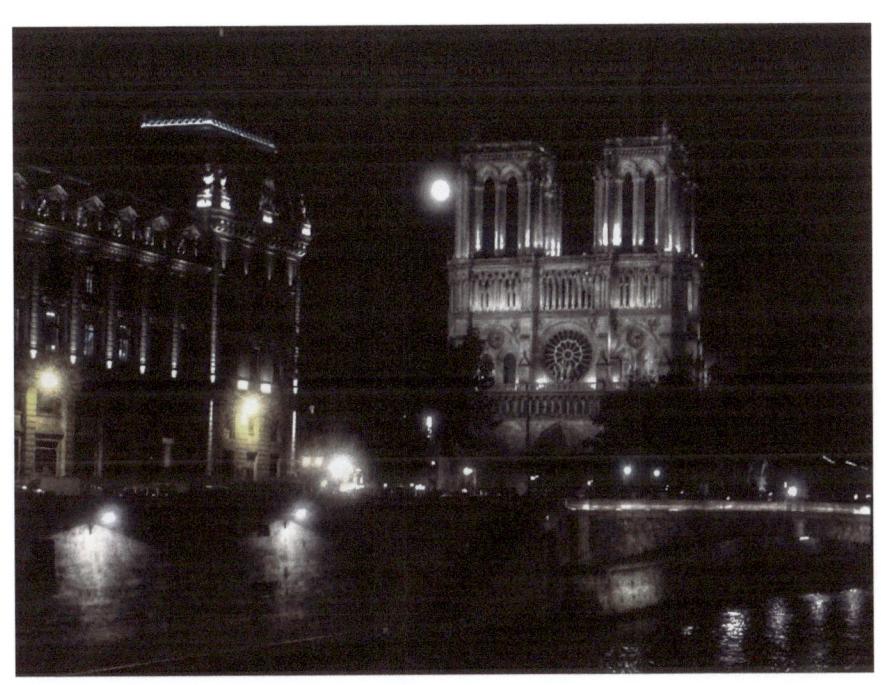

"America is my country, and Paris is my home town."

--Gertrude Stein

ACKNOWLEDGMENTS

For supporting and encouraging the trips that made these photos possible, heartfelt thanks to Vilay, Laura, Sally, Linda, Lea, Lyn, Ricky, Marilyn, Claudia, Michael, and MRM. And to the people in the pictures, all due respect – and that's a lot.

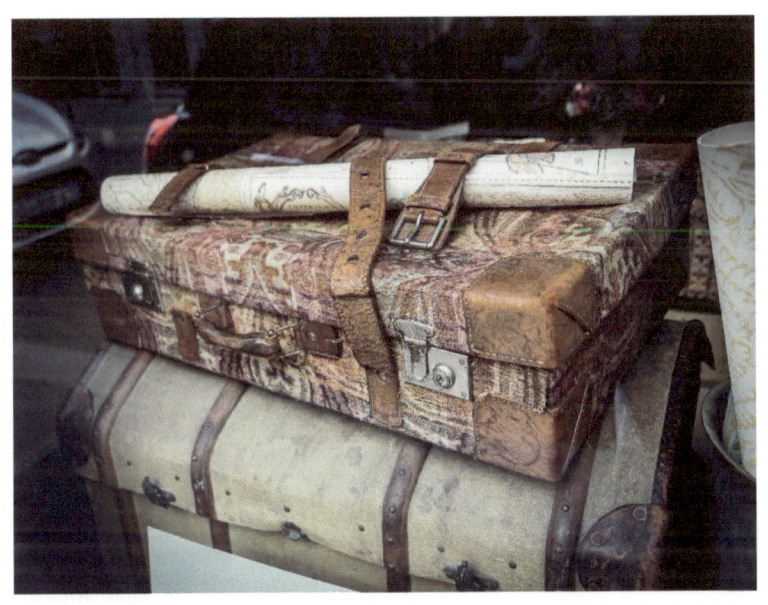

INTRODUCTION

I first visited Paris as a backpacking college kid in 1974, the summer Nixon resigned. Today as I await the withering of another US presidency, I am shocked to realize that as a young person, I was not smitten with the City of Light. I'm not sure why. It could have been the lumpy hotel bed and the toilet down the dark hall. It could have been the old rattly metro cars and Parisians' cool glances at these young American tourists with our unwieldy backpacks, ugly pants and sensible shoes. It could have been any number of things and, honestly, my indifference reveals questionable taste and judgment. I did not have the cultural courage to understand the raw, still postwar, very French Paris. I preferred London and Munich (talk about postwar – but we didn't get as far as West Berlin). Paris today is prettier, cleaner, more international. I revisited Paris in the mid-1990s and fell deeply, wholly and permanently in love.

These photos reflect fifteen years of frequent visits to Paris. They are a tiny selection of thousands of shots taken with all sorts of cameras and lenses, from a Canon DSLR to a long series of iPhones. (The earliest pictures here are around 2002, I think. They are film photos later digitized.) Paris has taught me that the camera doesn't matter. You can sneak up on people with a long lens or you can tug your phone out of your pocket to grab a shot. Paris is always a good idea, as the screenwriter put it, and always photogenic.

As I write this, I don't live in Paris, but whenever I arrive in the city, I am home. At Charles de Gaulle airport, I've learned not to stumble on the bouncy conveyer belt that takes us to our luggage – even after a night of no sleep, in my giddy relief at landing east of the Atlantic. Like my earlier failure to appreciate Paris's magnetism, my comfort today is a mystery. My French is sparse. I don't dress like Parisian women of my age. Although I try to blend in, I am spotted as an American the minute I walk into a shop or up to a museum counter, even though I call out "Bonjour, madame/monsieur!" as one must do (maybe that's it). Waiters simply ask what I want in their school-taught English.

But I know the smells and sounds of the city. I know how to buy metro tickets and how to find my platform. I know where to look for the itinerant orchestra on Sunday afternoon. I know how to avoid the street scams. I know where the toilets are. One day a family from the suburbs asked me for directions – another day, some German tourists. They may all have been desperate, but I don't care. An elderly French woman asked me to help her cross the street, and we chatted for a while in my rusty AP French. Another Parisian woman saw me gazing at the domes on the Orthodox cathedral in the 7e and told me an apocryphal tale of its construction ("the Russians wanted it to be as tall as the Eiffel Tower!").

I walk for miles. I jog up and down stone stairs and wander over cobbles by the Seine. I try to memorize the names of all the bridges – it's really about time I knew them all. I stay in apartments but my imagination moves me into every hotel, trying on the rooms and service for size. I go to the museums and galleries and daydream my way through them. I window shop but rarely buy. I look and look and look. I am at the center of the world. I don't need anything else.

I hope the photographs speak for themselves, but I also love words and so I added a verbal counterpoint to the images. I borrowed the words of others. Not all the writers speak for me, but they all speak in strong, sure tones.

The photographer was lucky to catch the moments that follow. It may be that when people get to Paris, they live the lives they want to live, with their lovers or their children or their Tai Chi pals. They don't look around to see who's photographing them. Who cares? They are in Paris.

The guys in red, in the fountain? I'll tell you in the next book.

Corvallis, Oregon

October 2018

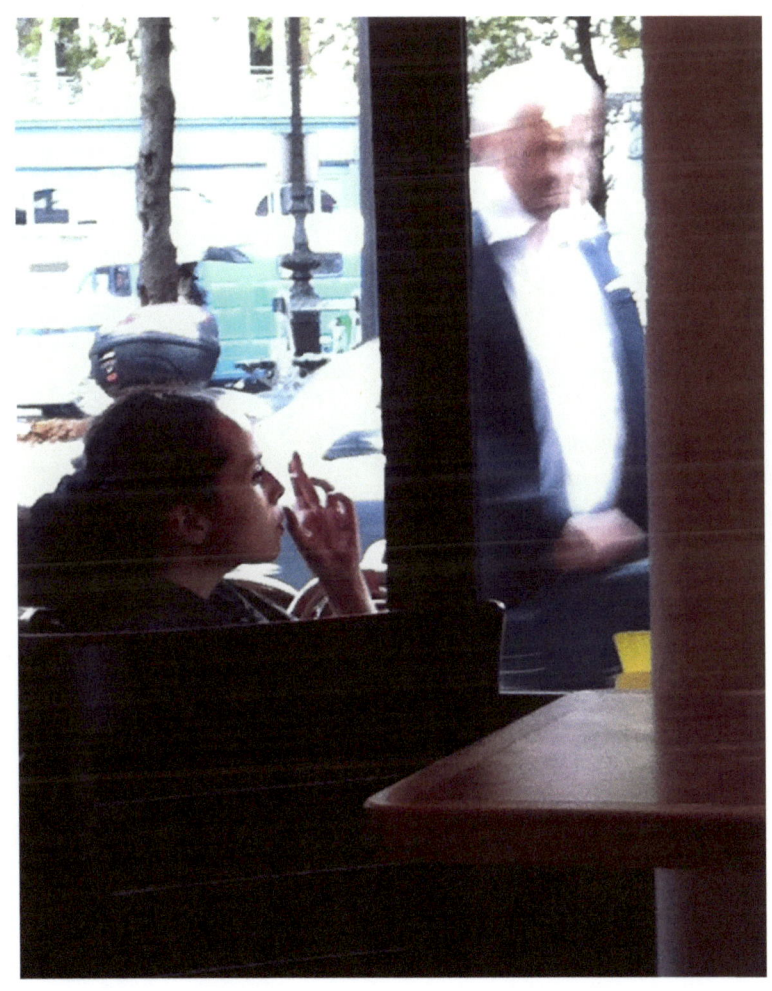

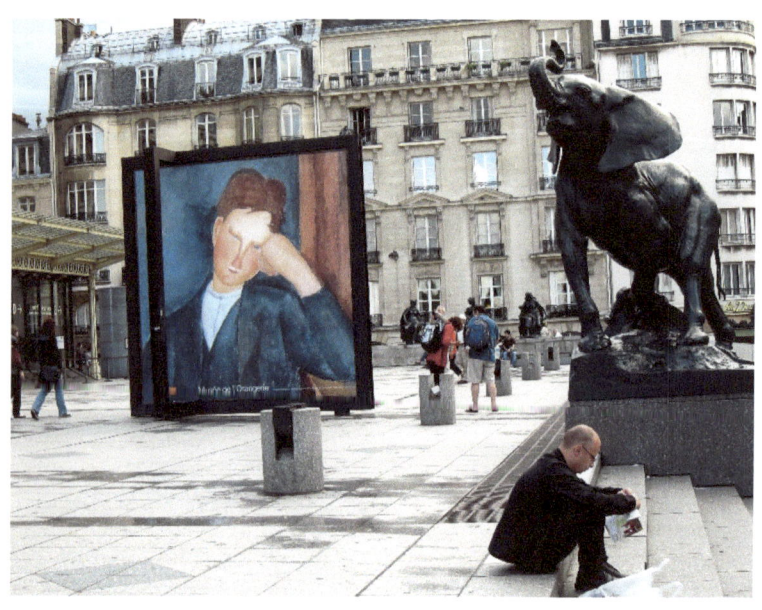

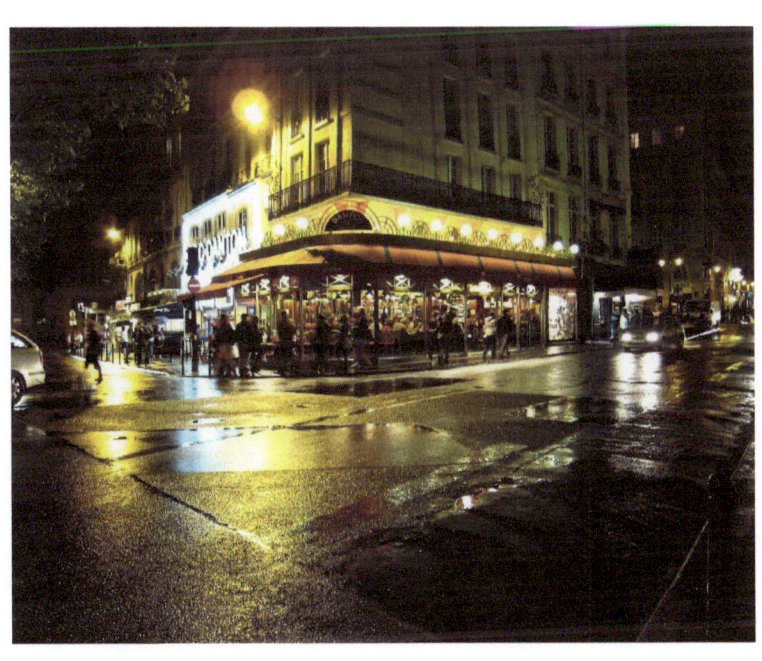

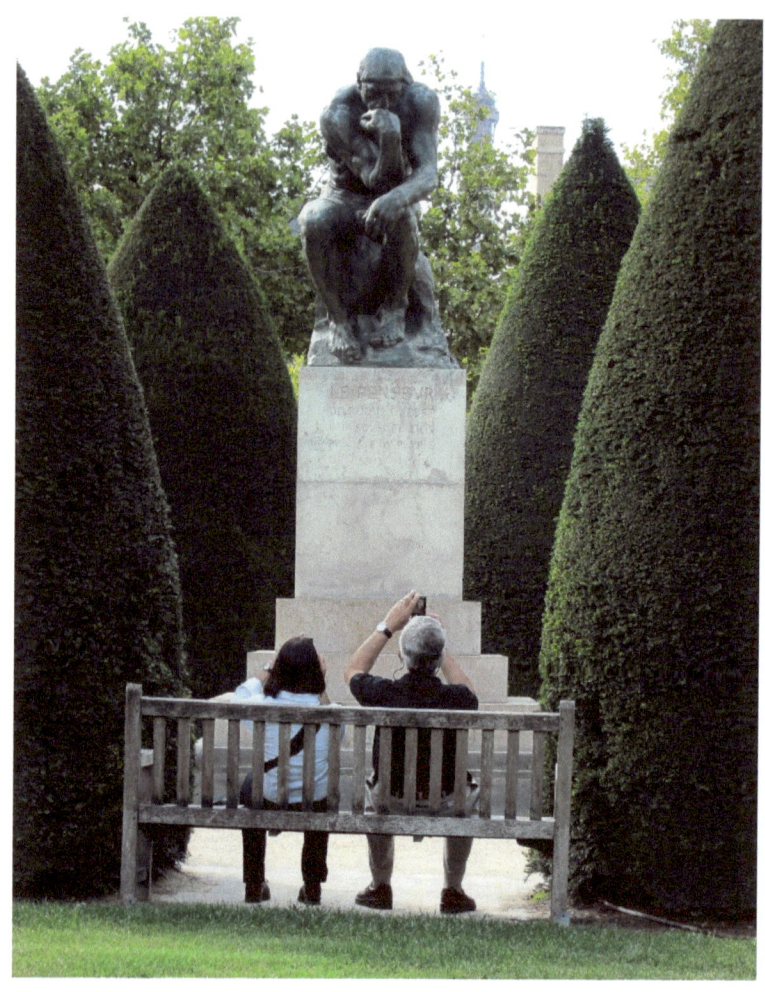

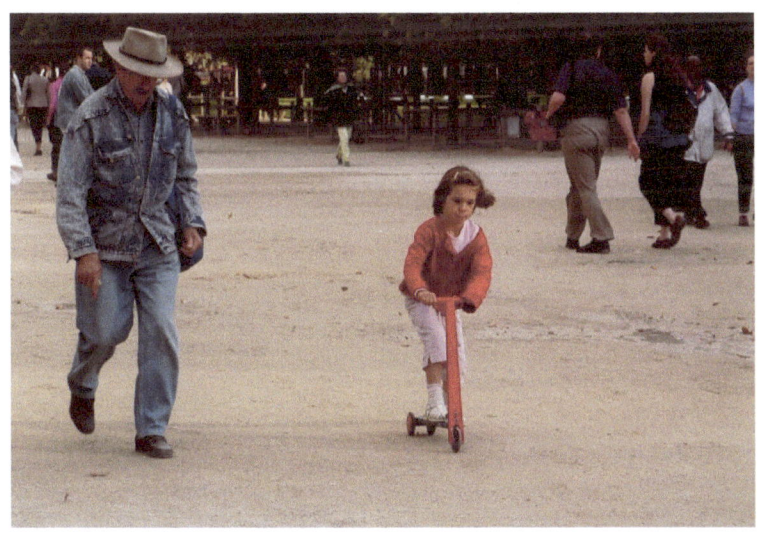

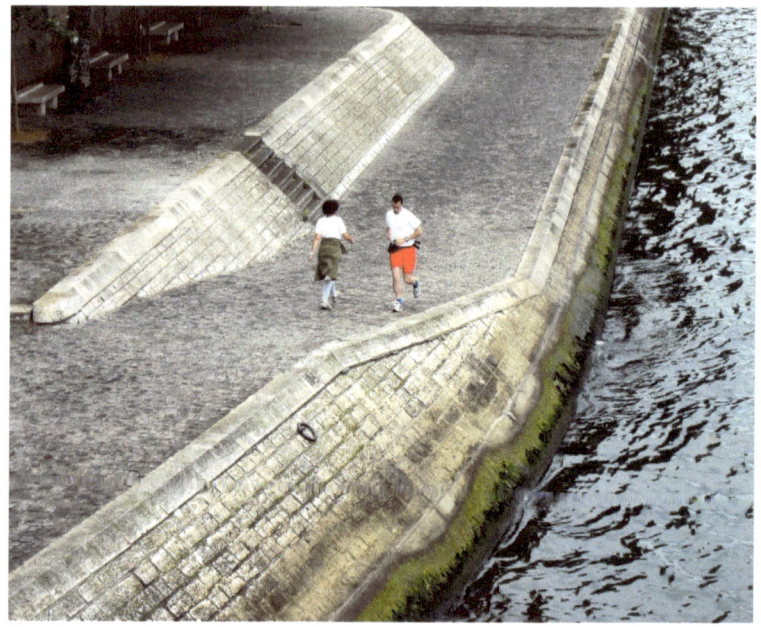

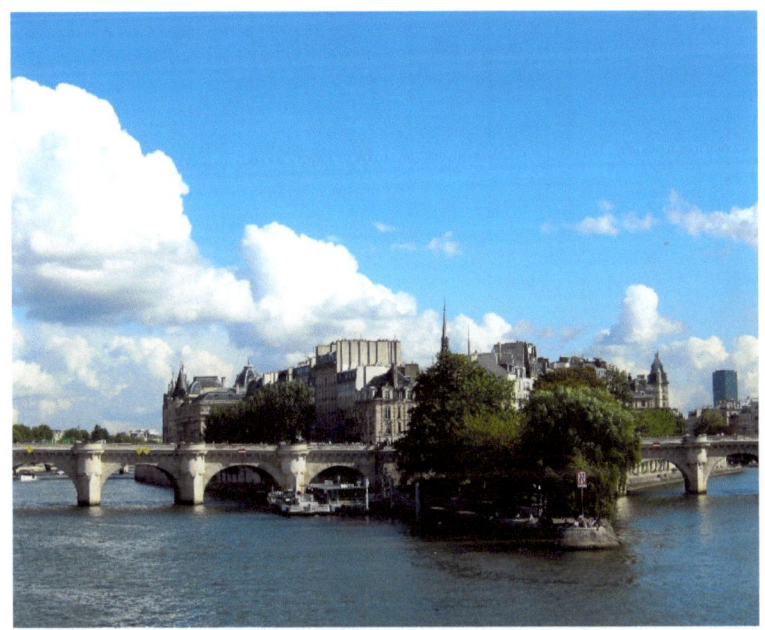

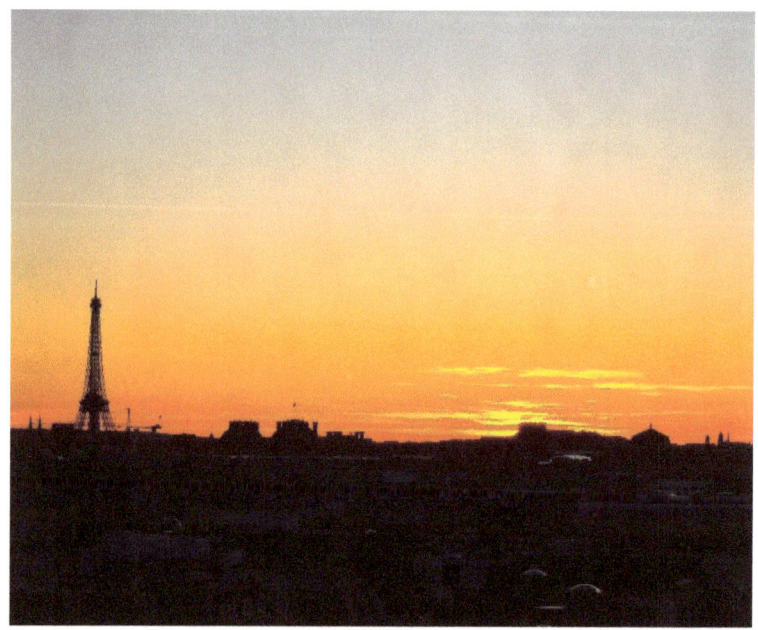

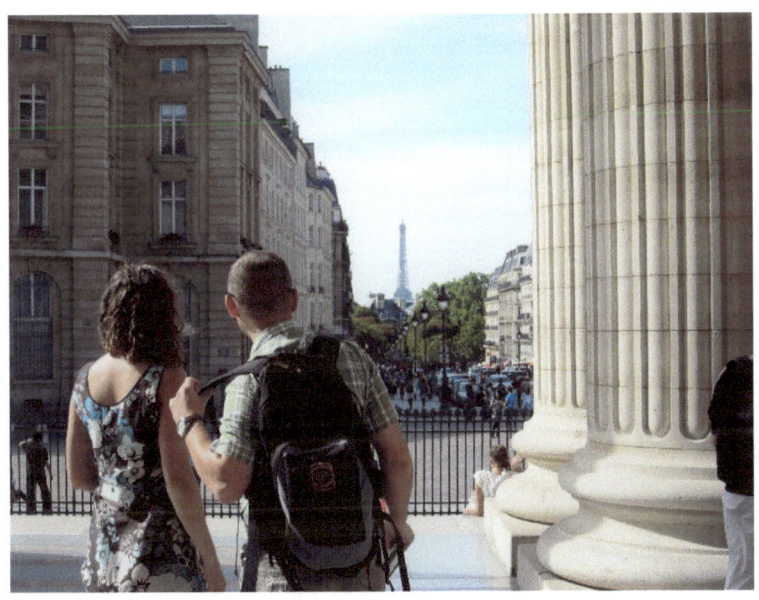

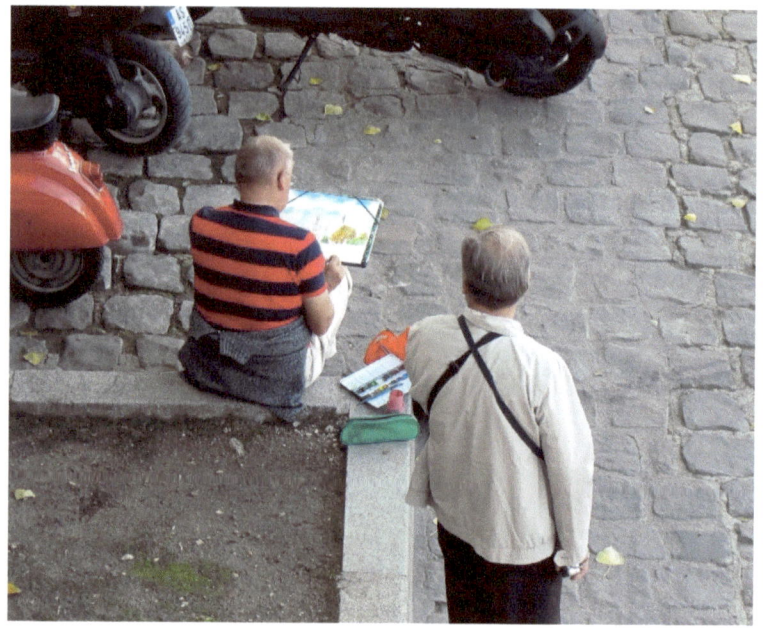

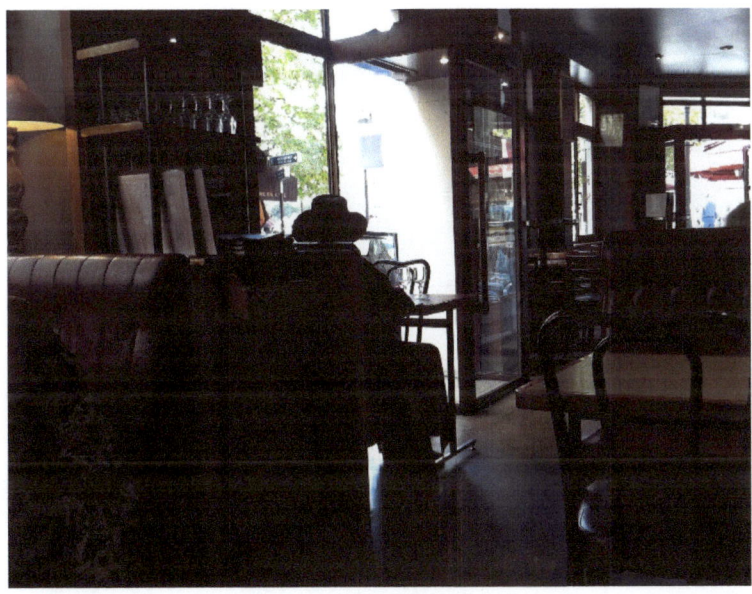

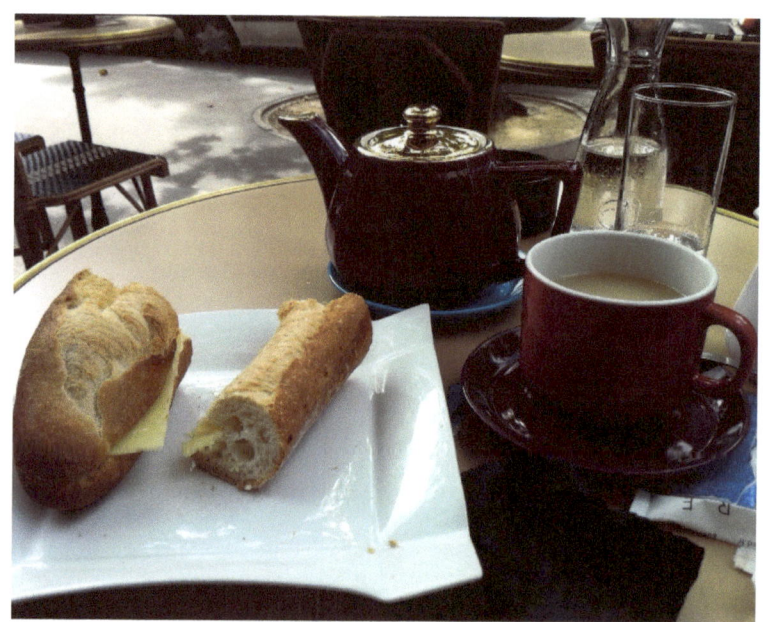

"I have always highly esteemed the brave and humble workers who labor all night to produce those soft but crusty loaves that look more like cake than bread."

--Alexandre Dumas

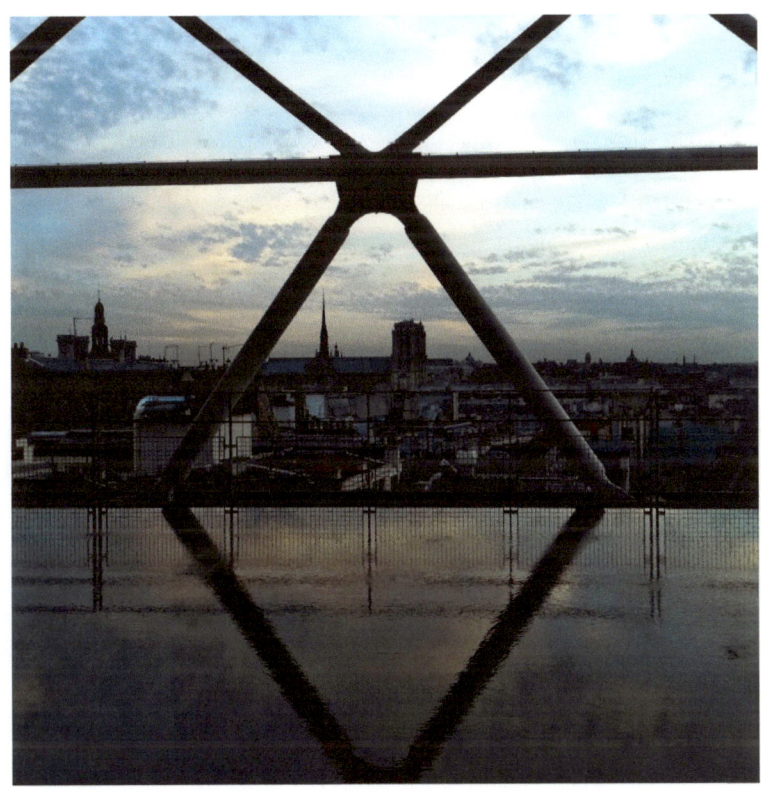

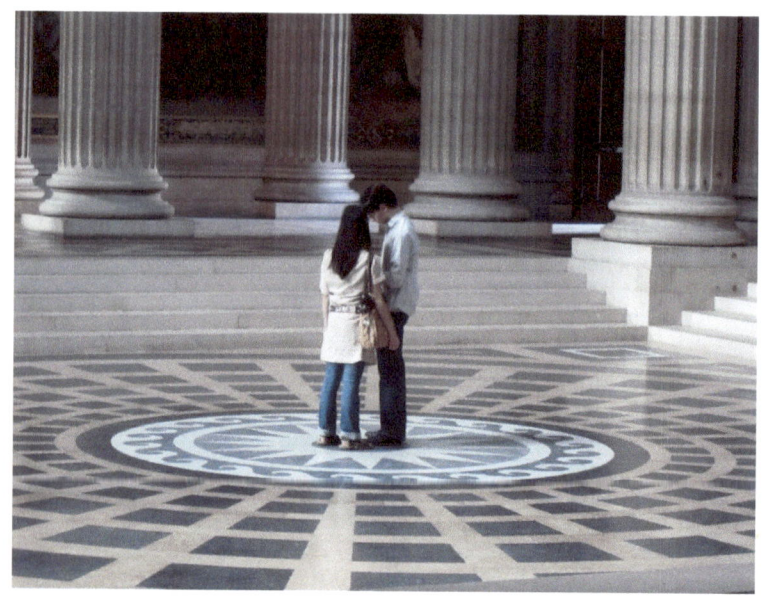

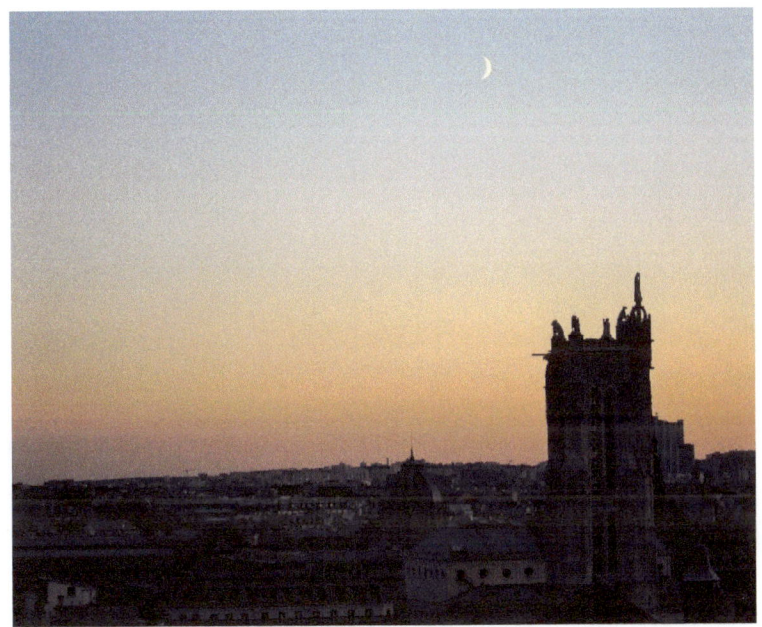

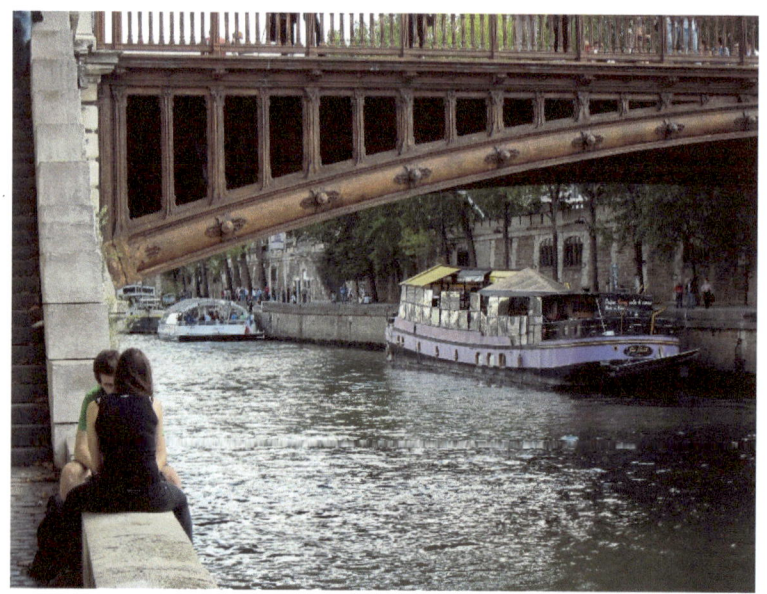

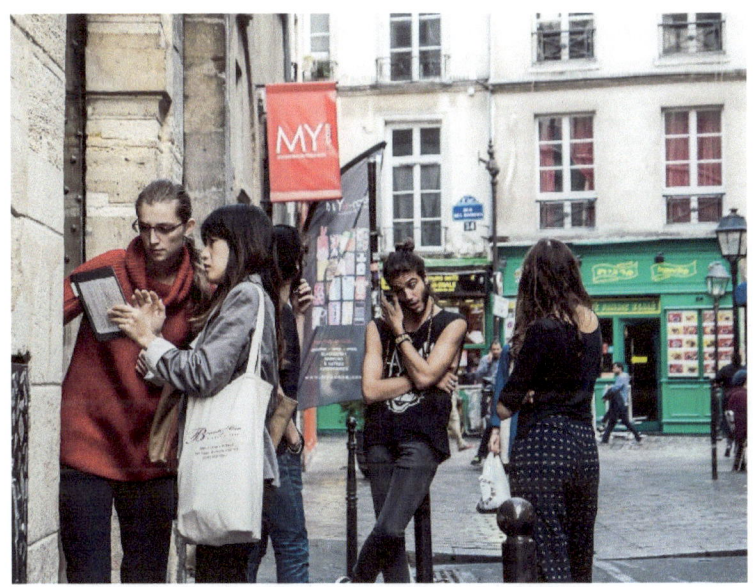

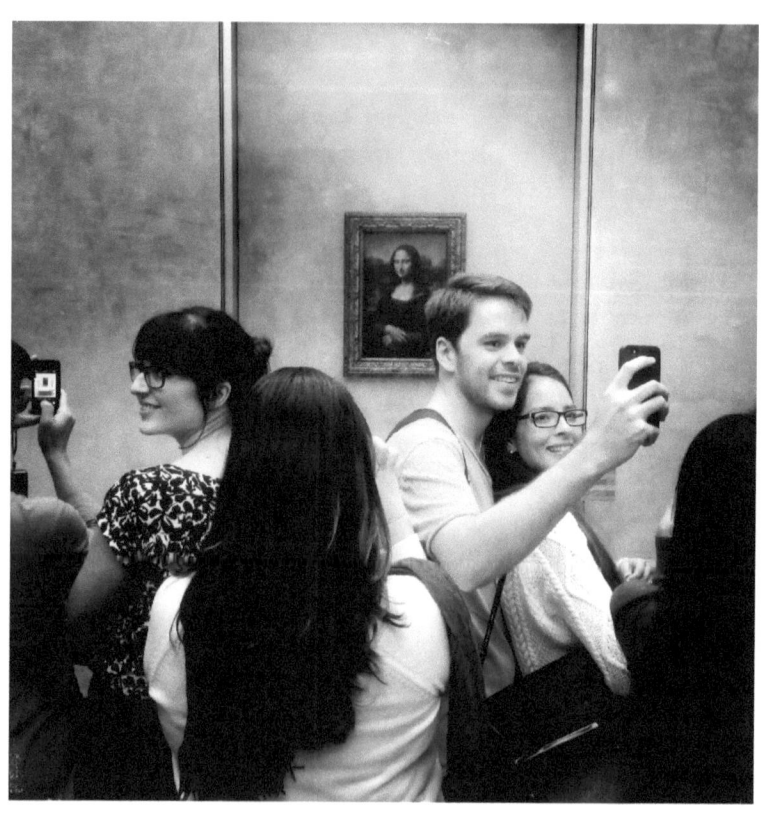

"What's the name of that famous museum in Paris? The Louvre? I went through that place in 20 minutes."

--Peter Falk

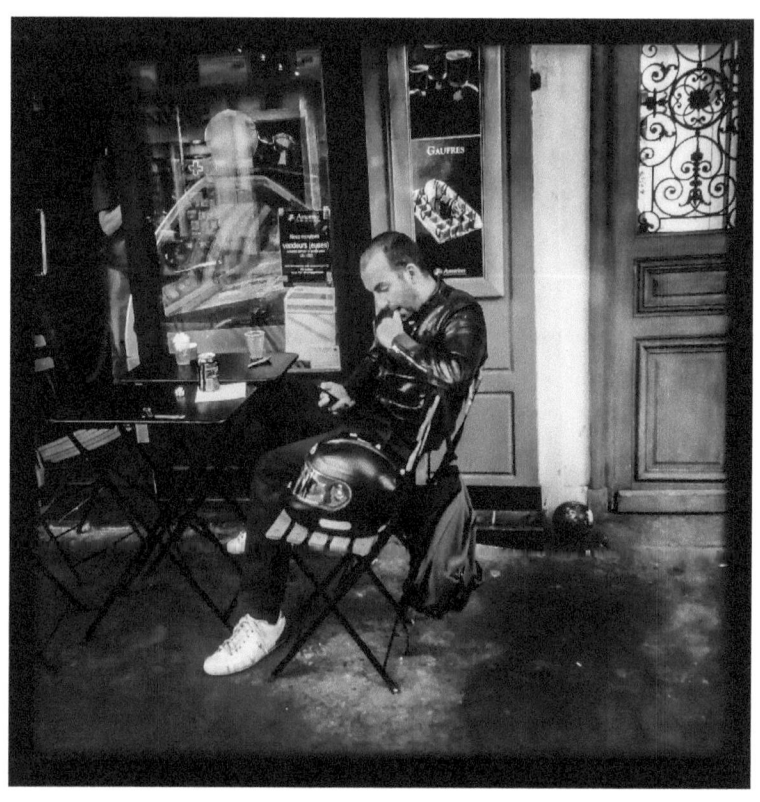

"If you are lucky enough to have lived in Paris as a young man, then wherever you go for the rest of your life it stays with you, for Paris is a moveable feast."

--Ernest Hemingway

"Little by little, the old world crumbled, and not once did the king imagine that some of the pieces might fall on him."

--Jennifer Donnelly

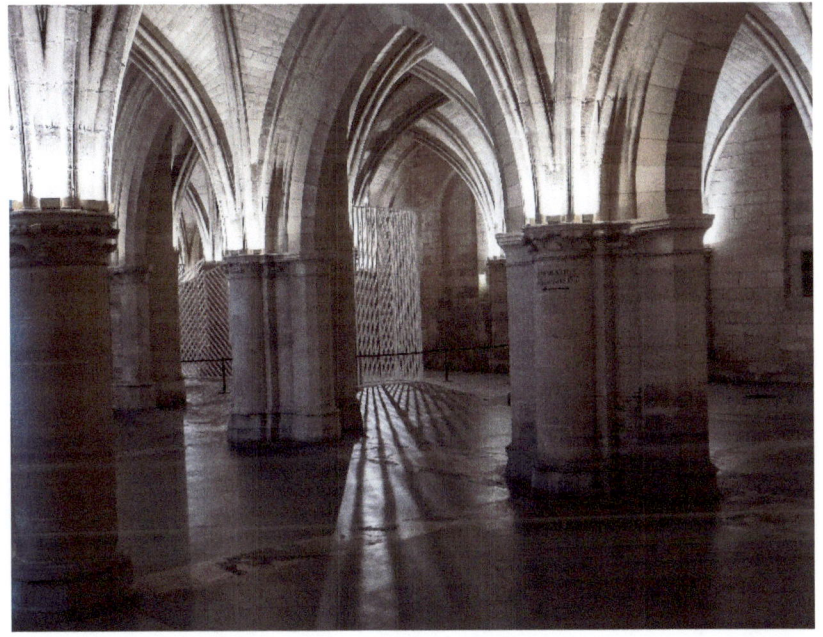

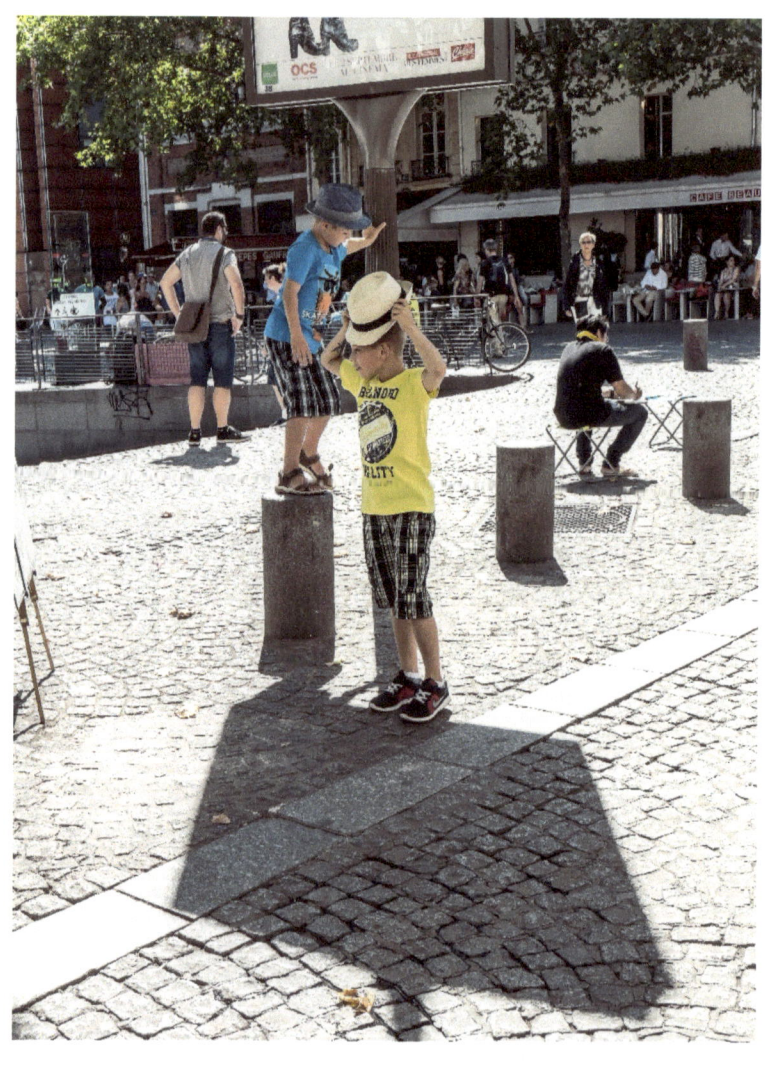

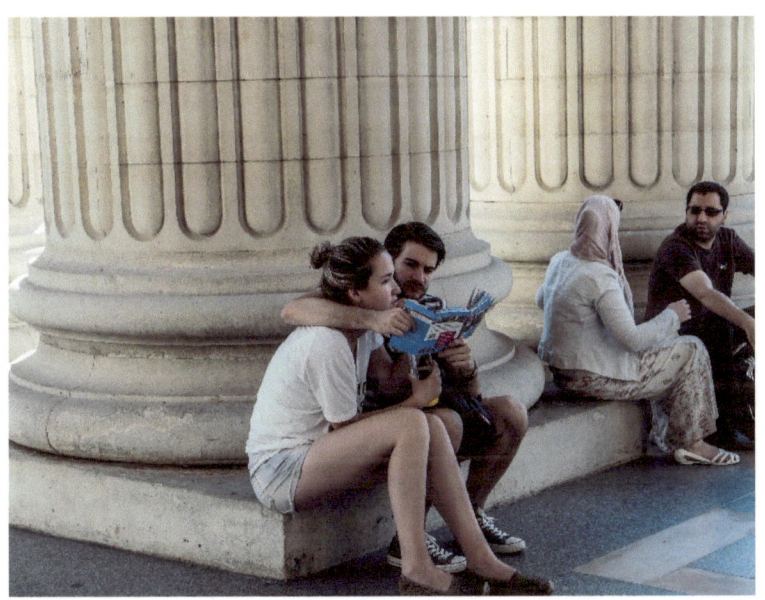

"We'll always have Paris."

--Julius and Philip Epstein, Howard Koch

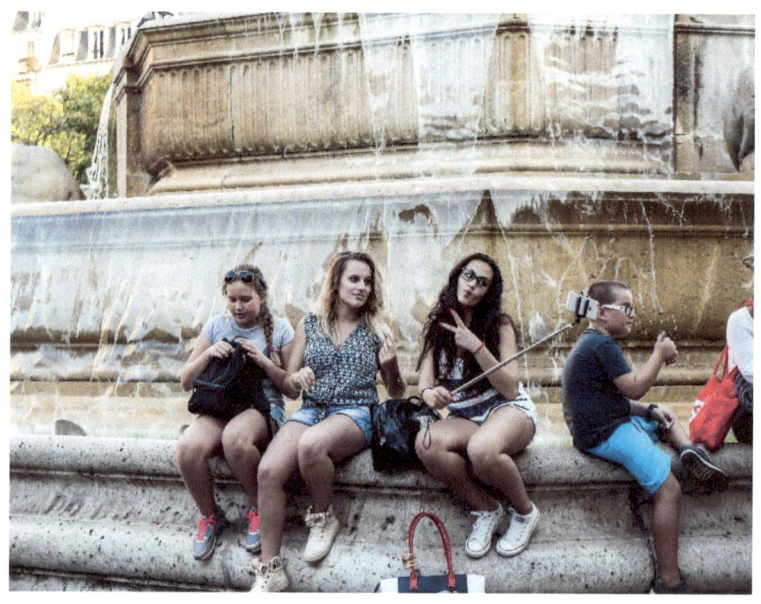

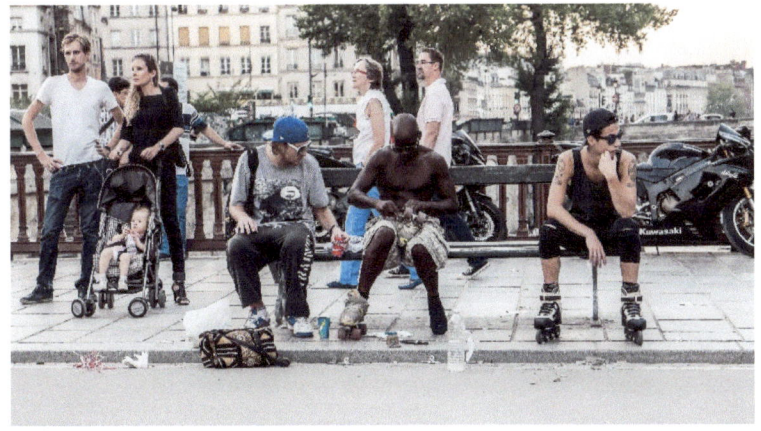

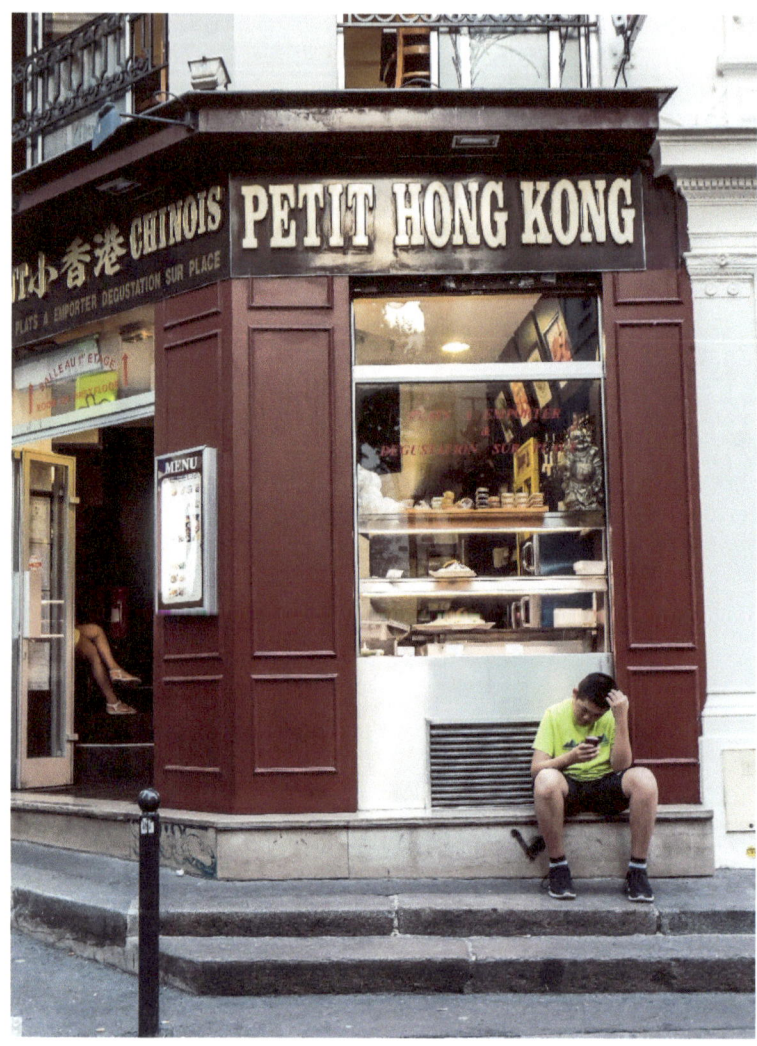

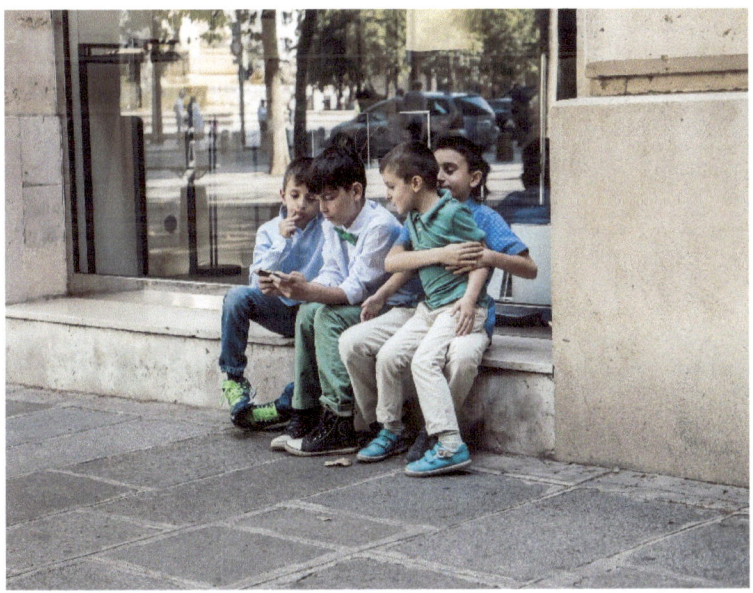

"Paris was all so…Parisian. I was captivated by the wonderful wrongness of it all – the unfamiliar fonts, the brand names in the supermarket. The dimensions of the bricks and paving stones. Children, really quite small children, speaking fluent French!"

--David Nicholls

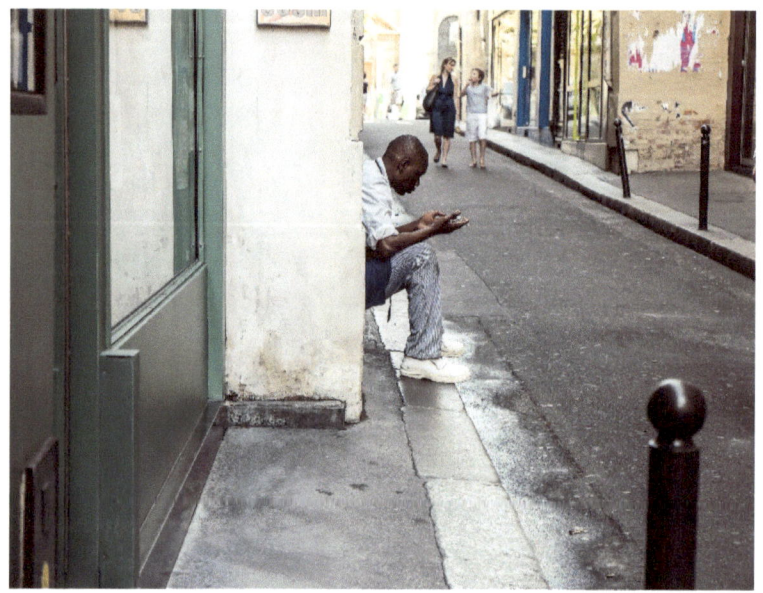

"If you ask the great city, 'Who is this person?,' she will answer, 'He is my child.'"

--Victor Hugo

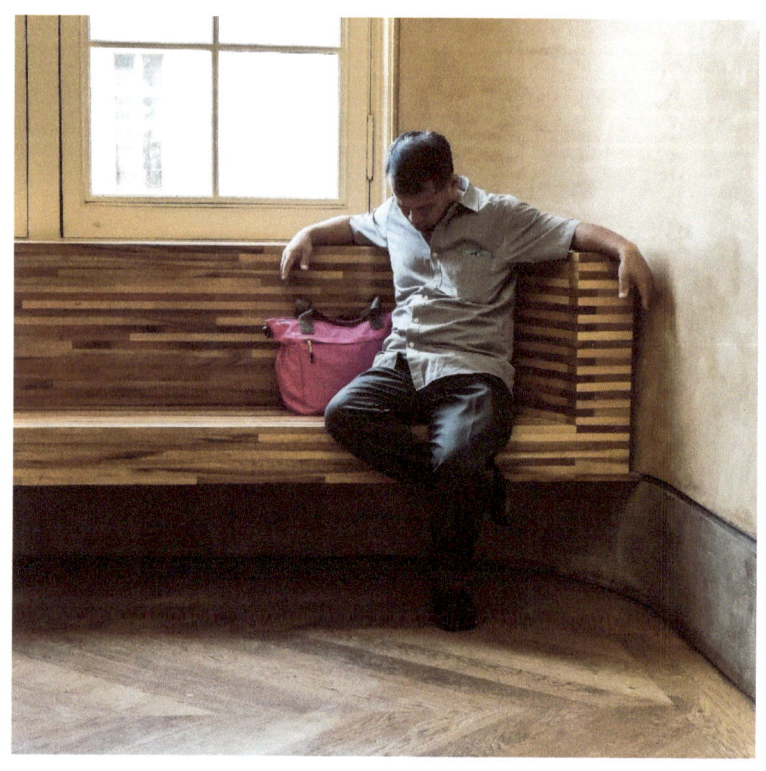

"It's big, it's grand, and I'm tired."

--Paul L

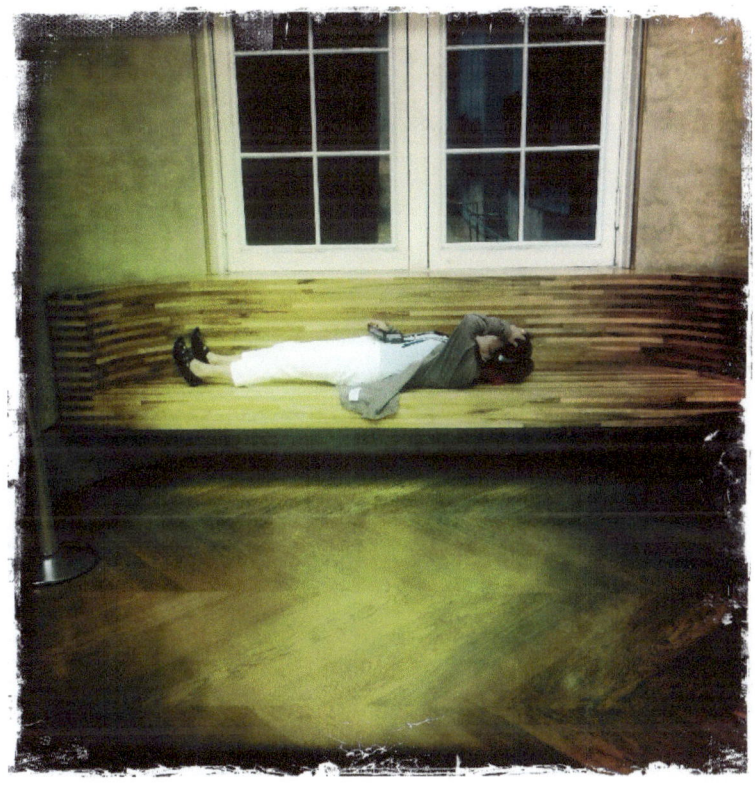

"The café is where you go to watch and be watched."

--Jetsetter

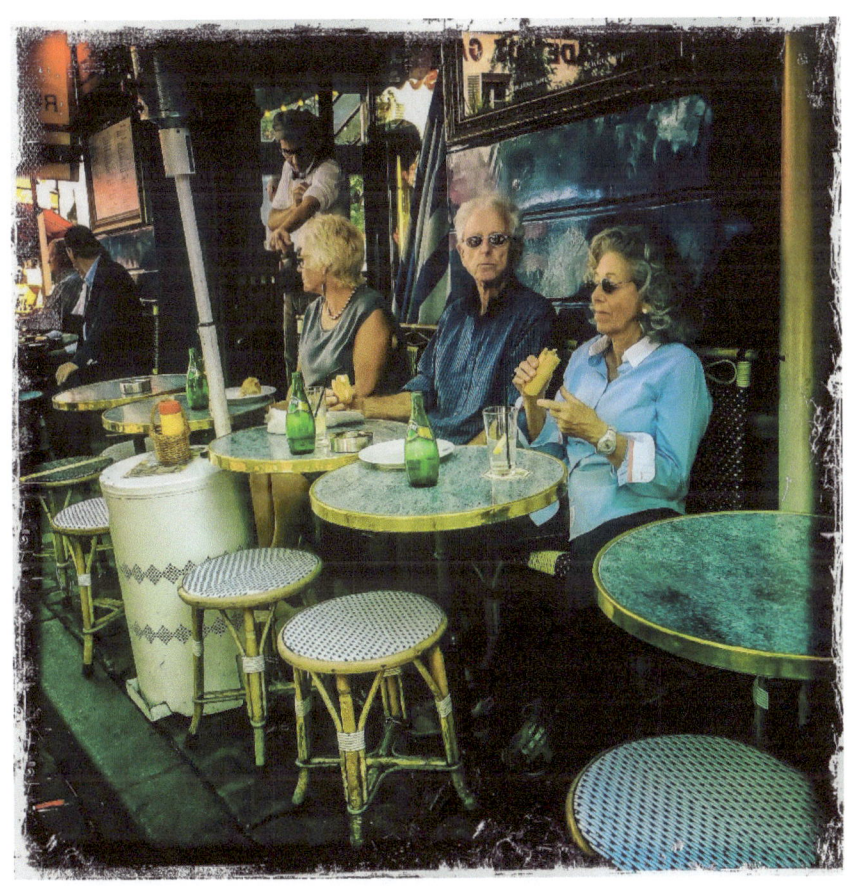

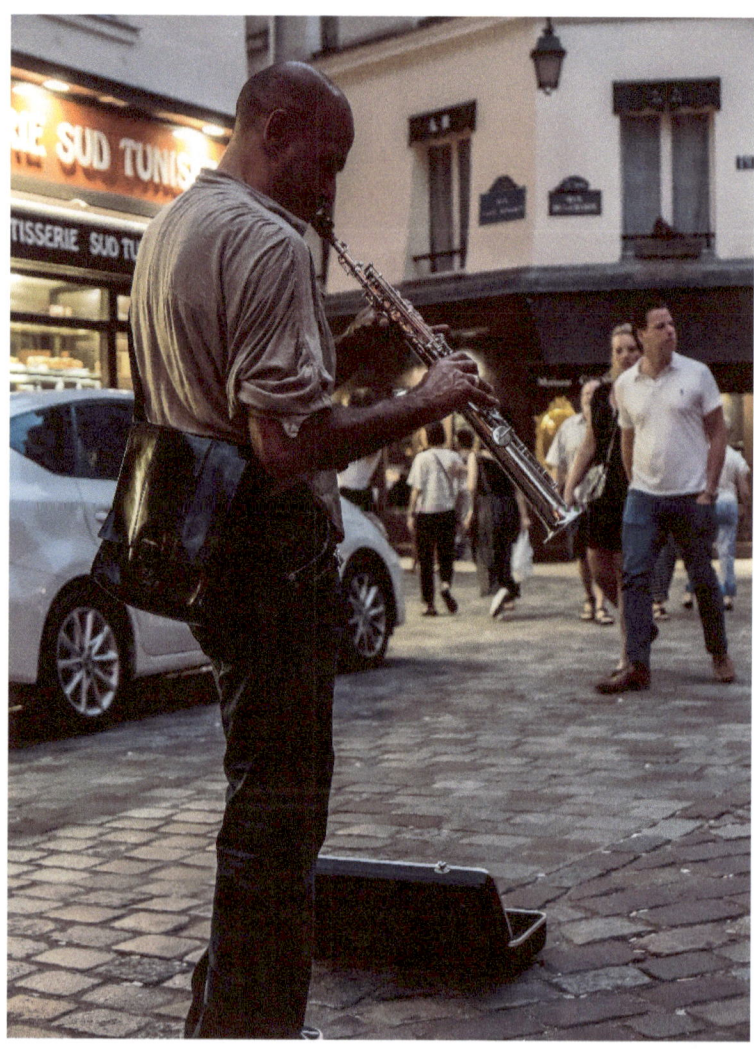

"When you busk, you're throwing yourself over to the unexpected."

--Mélissa

"I wish I could go to Paris right now."

--Emily J. Proctor

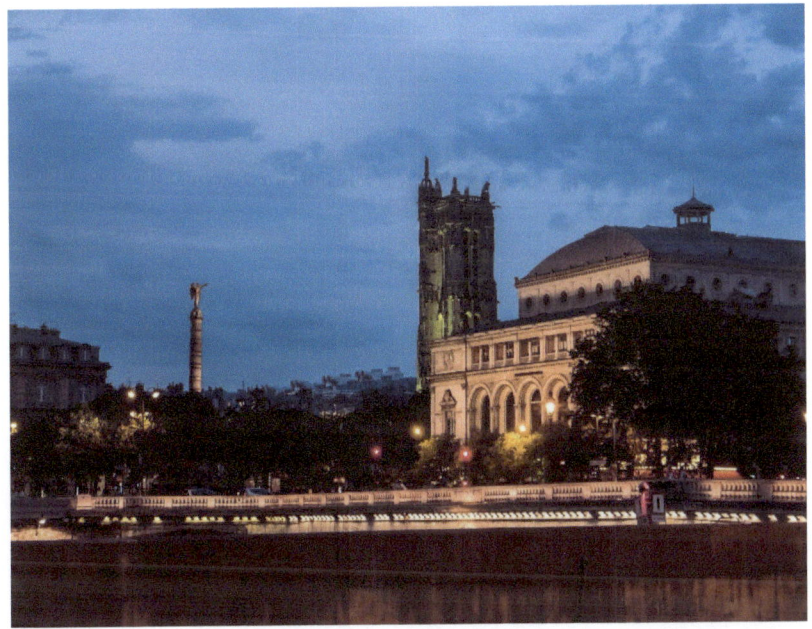

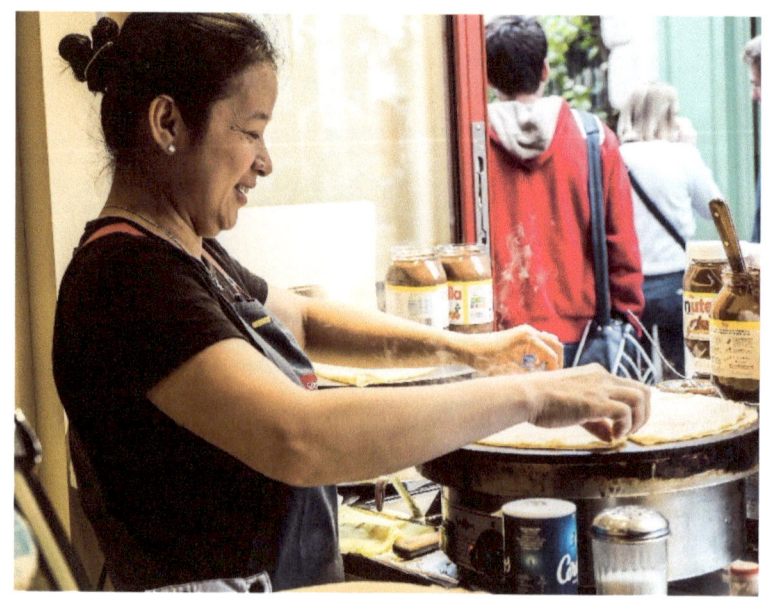

"Cook until the bottom of the crepe begins to brown and you can slide a spatula under it. It will hold together quite well, so you can flip it over pretty easily."

--King Arthur Flour

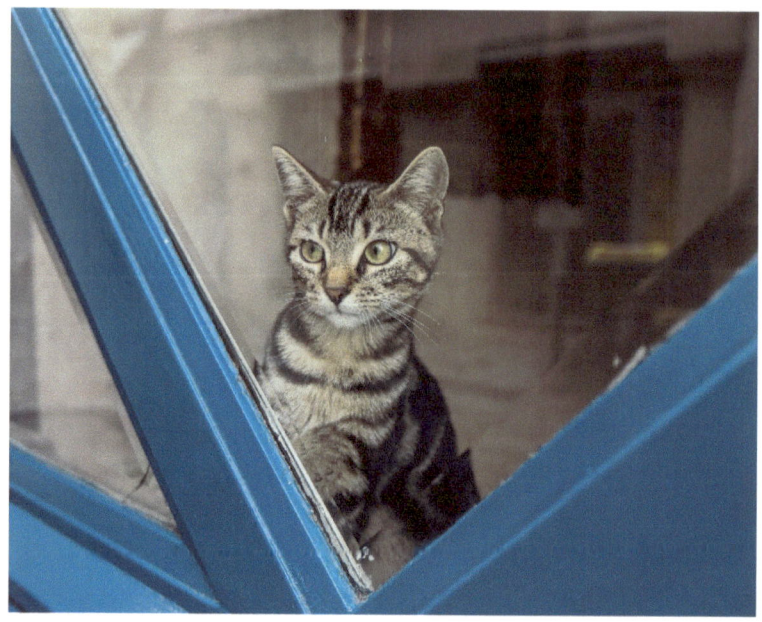

"They have hair groomed to perfection, eyes you can't say no to, and all the airs and graces of the French aristocracy."

--Clare McVay

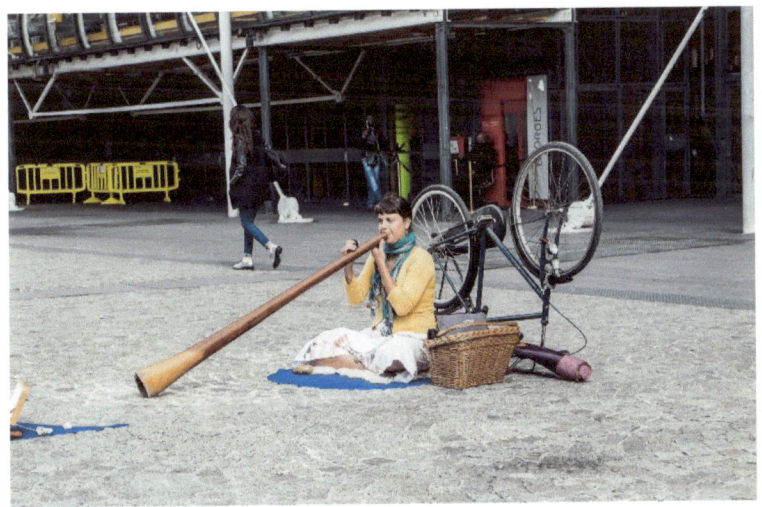

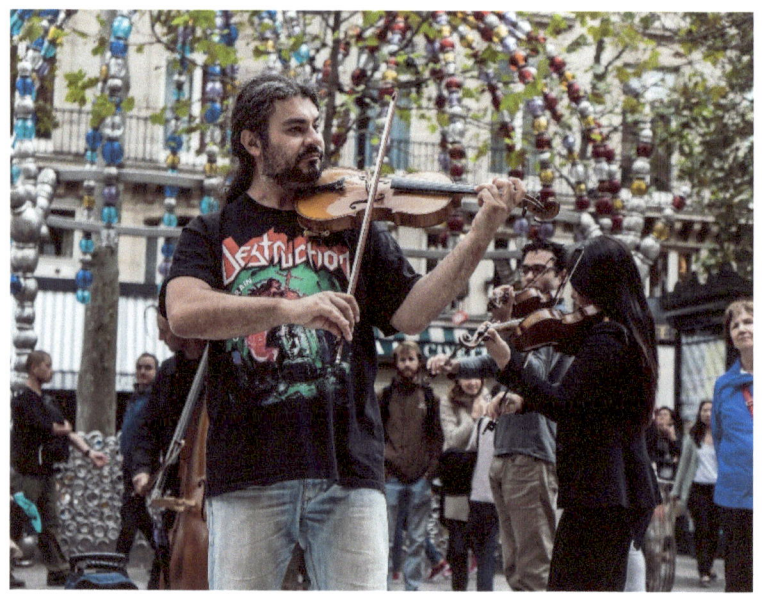

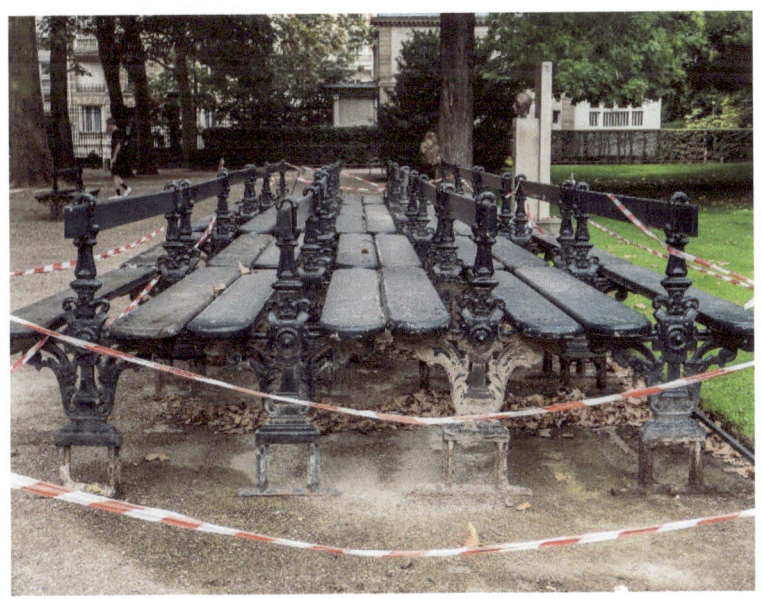

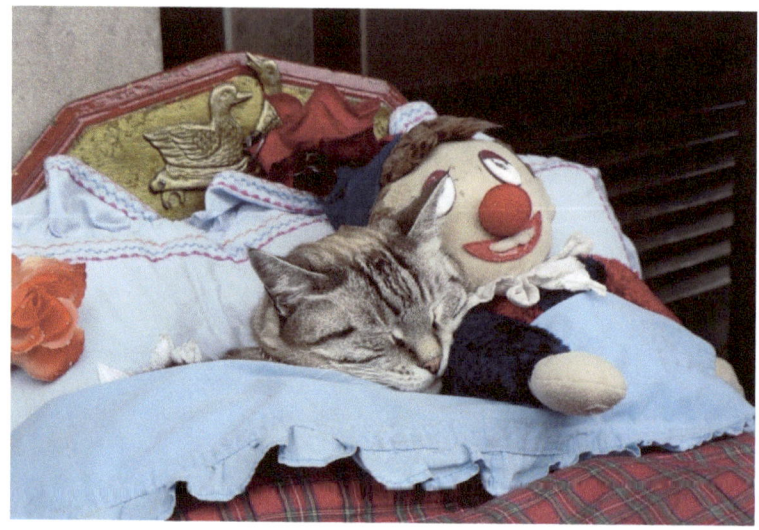

"It is a good thing to go to Paris for a few days if you have had a lot of trouble, and that is my advice to everyone except Parisians."

--Muriel Spark

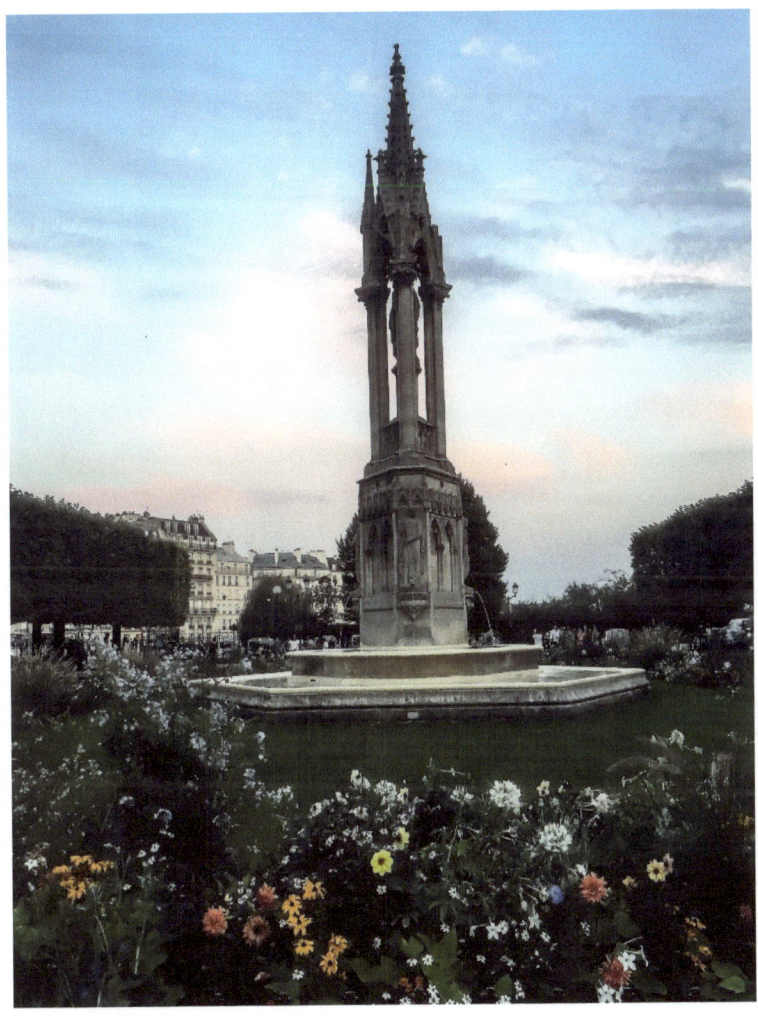

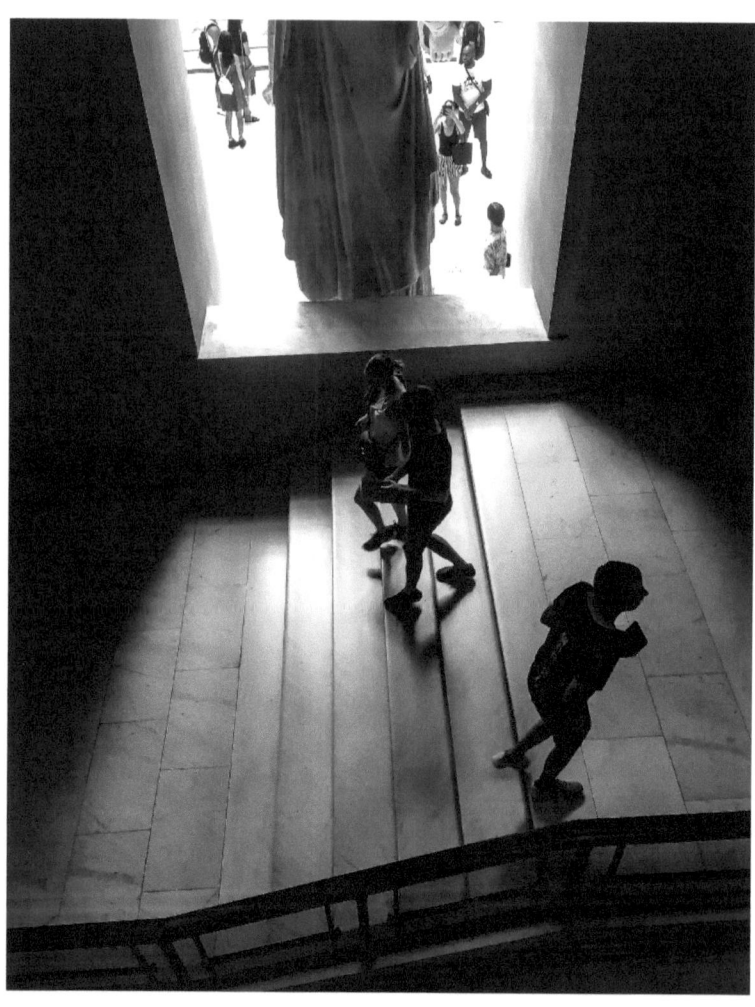

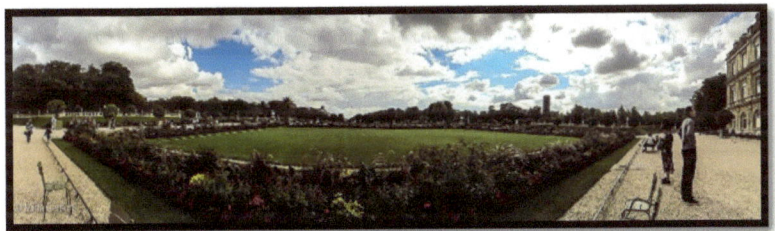

"After joyfully working each morning, I would leave off around midday to challenge myself to a footrace. Speeding along the sunny paths of the Jardin de Luxembourg, ideas would breed like aphids in my head – for creative invention is easy and sublime when air cycles quickly through the lungs and the body is busy at noble tasks."

--Roman Payne

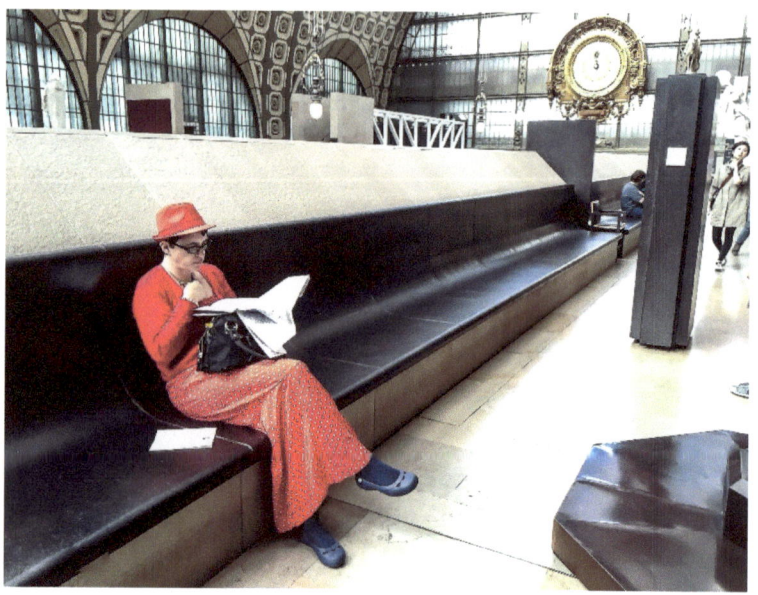

"I believe in walking out of a museum before the paintings you've seen begin to run together. How else can you carry anything away with you in your mind's eye?"
— Elizabeth Kostova

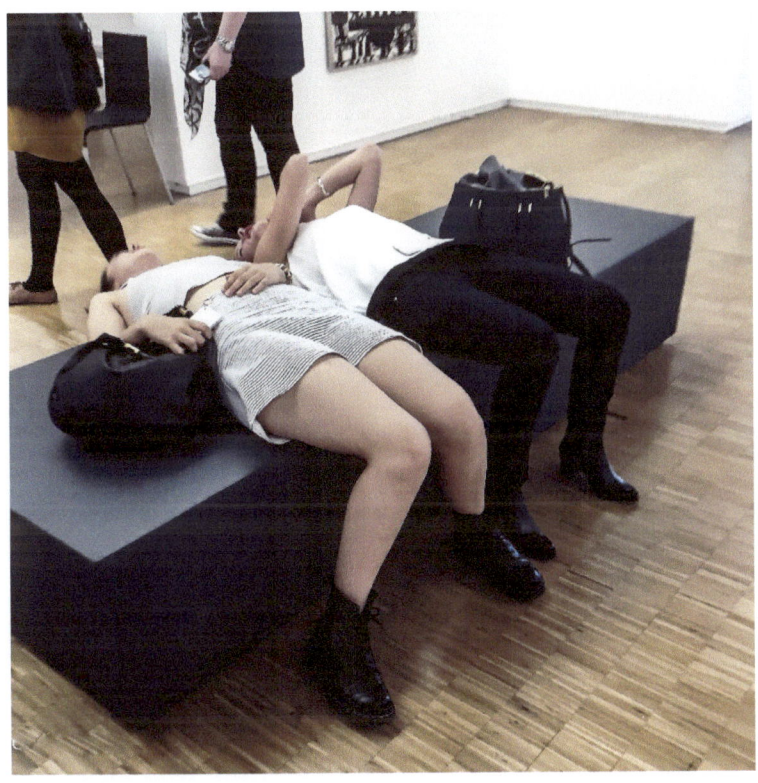

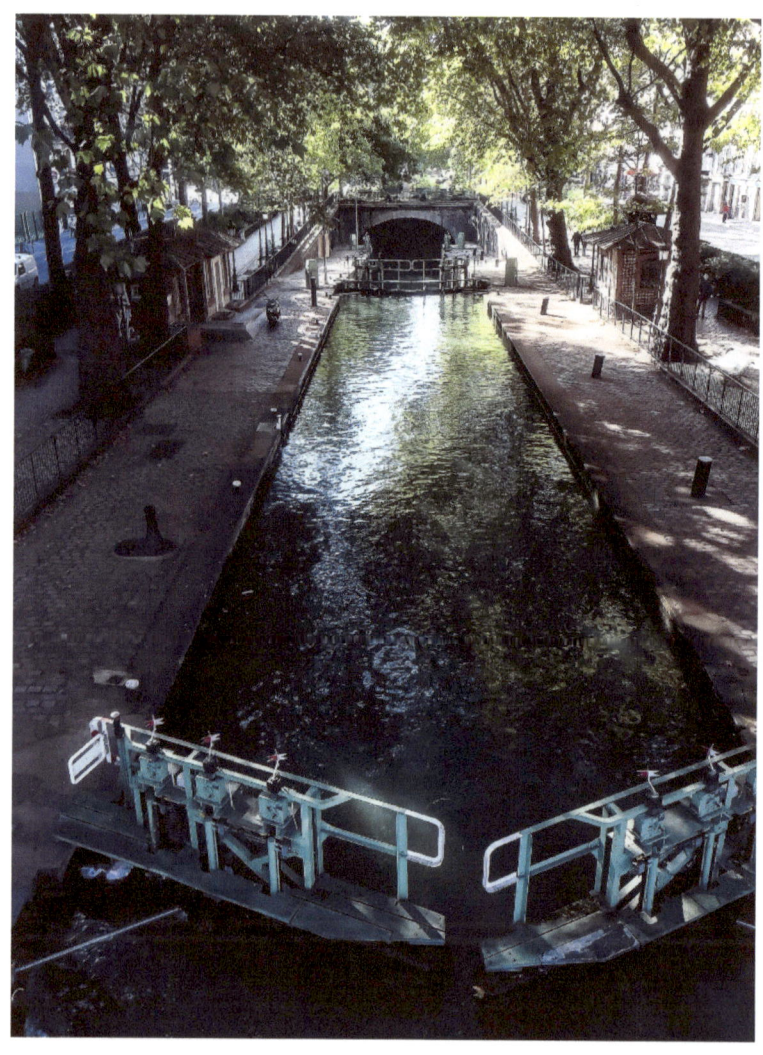

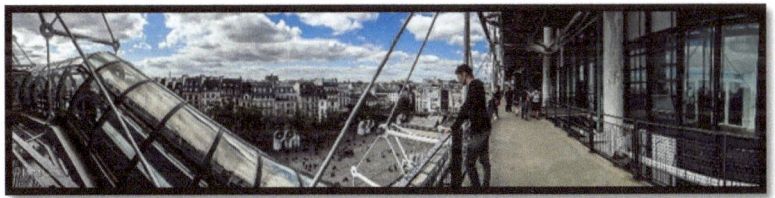

"Mine was the twilight and the morning. Mine was a world of rooftops and love songs."
--Roman Payne

Mina Carson

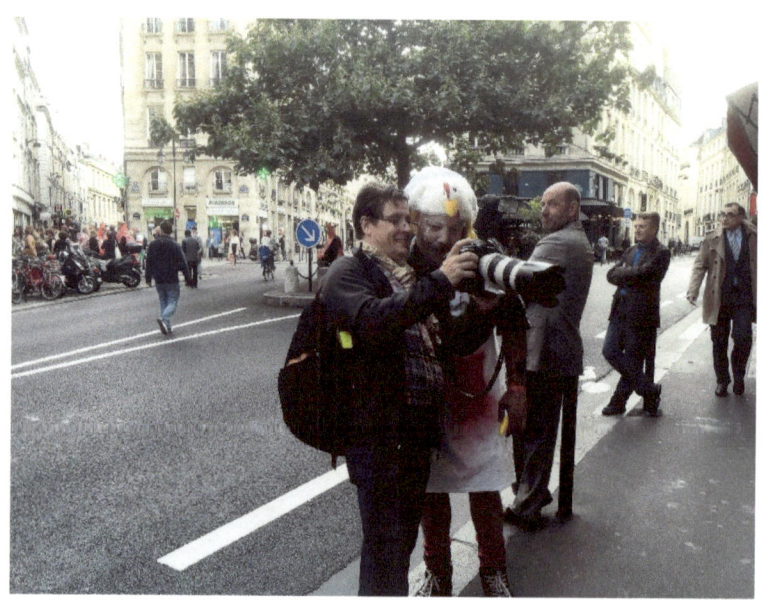

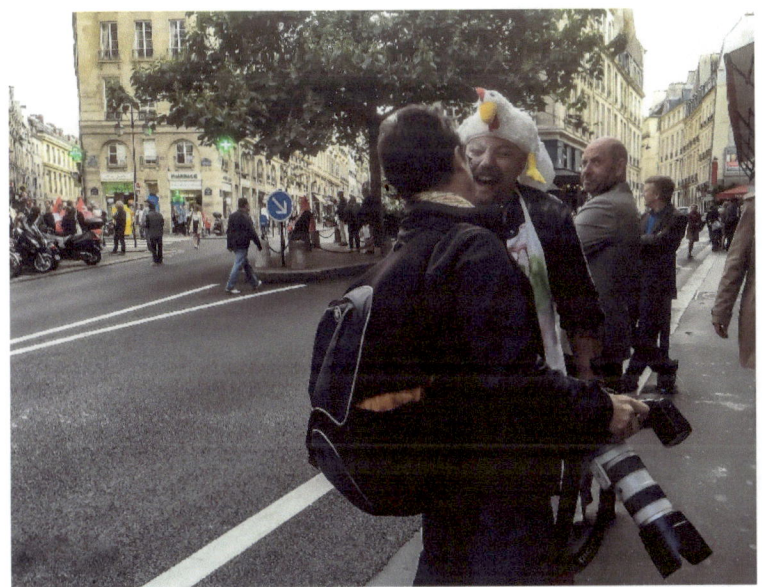

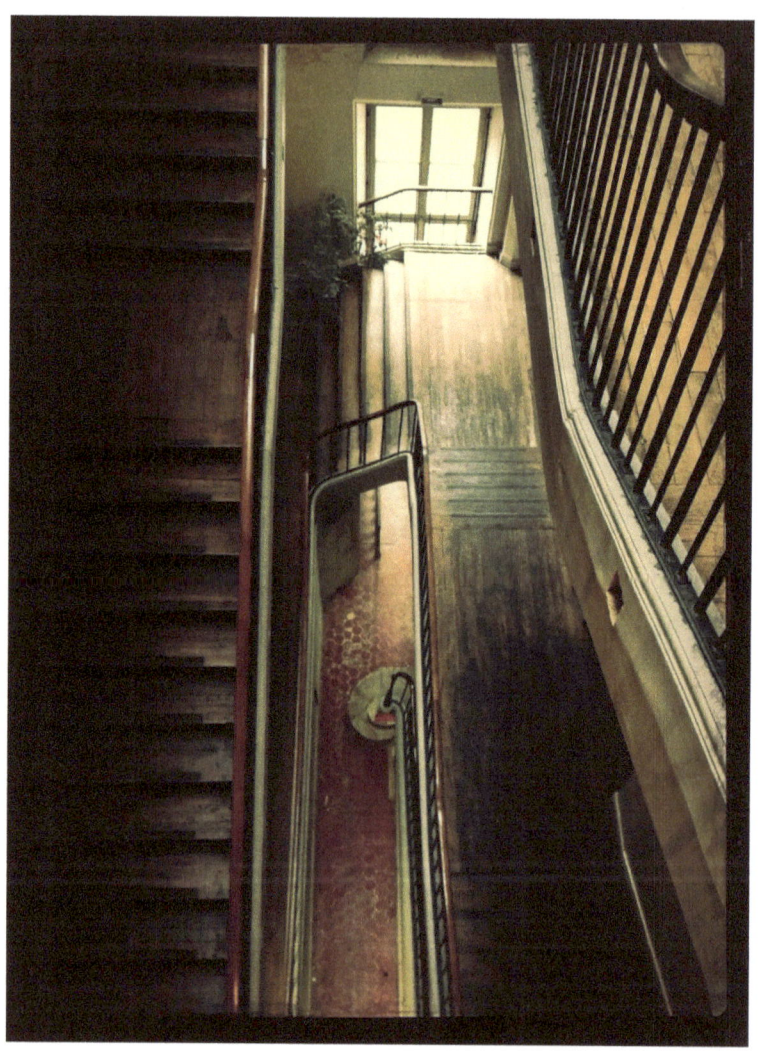

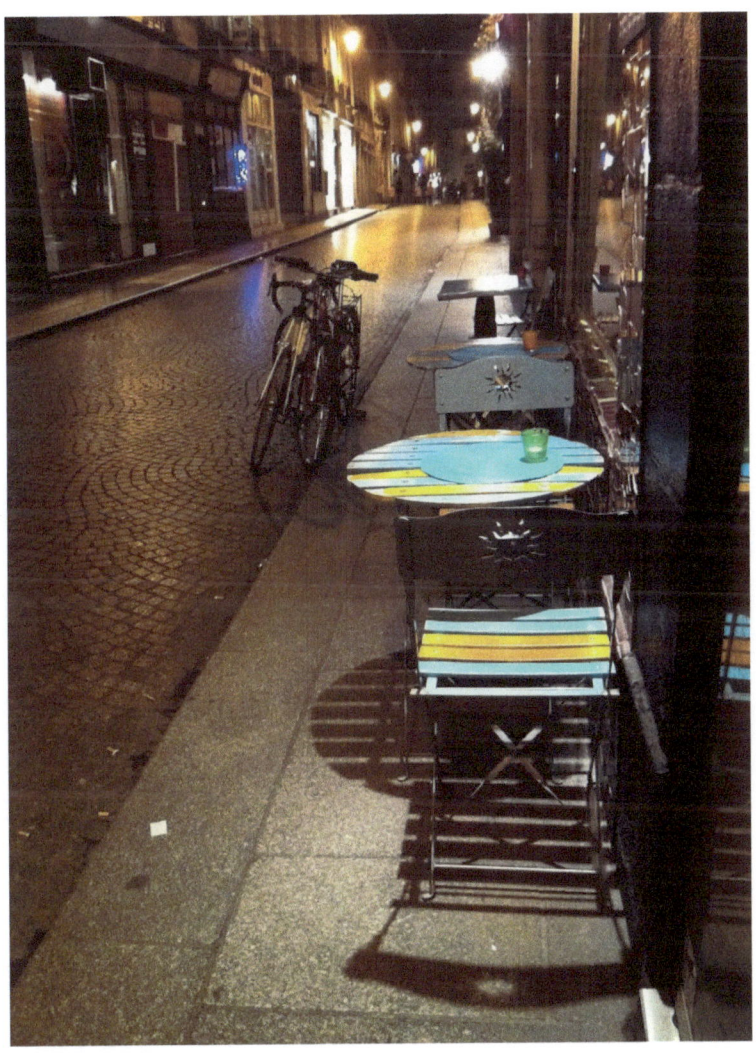

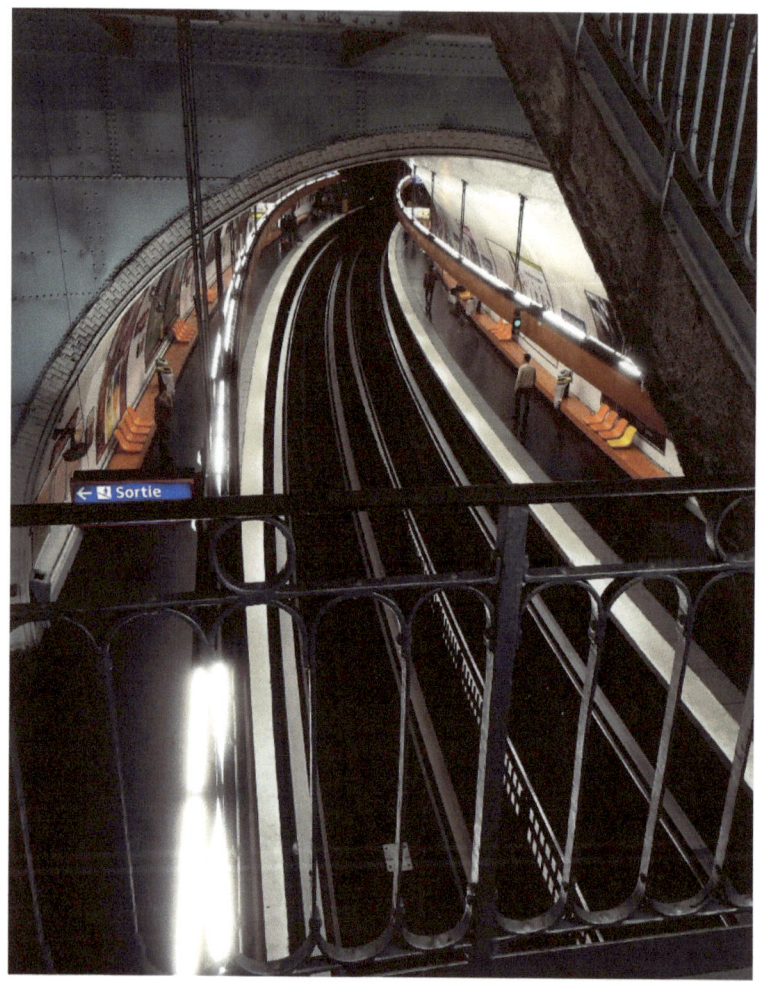

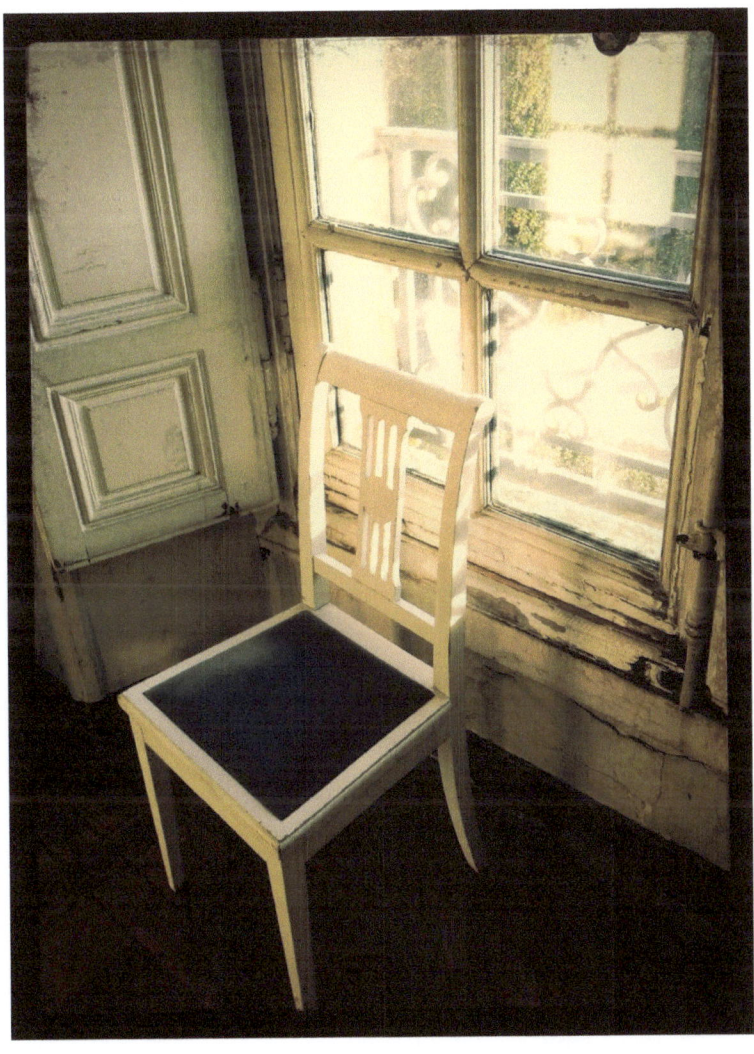

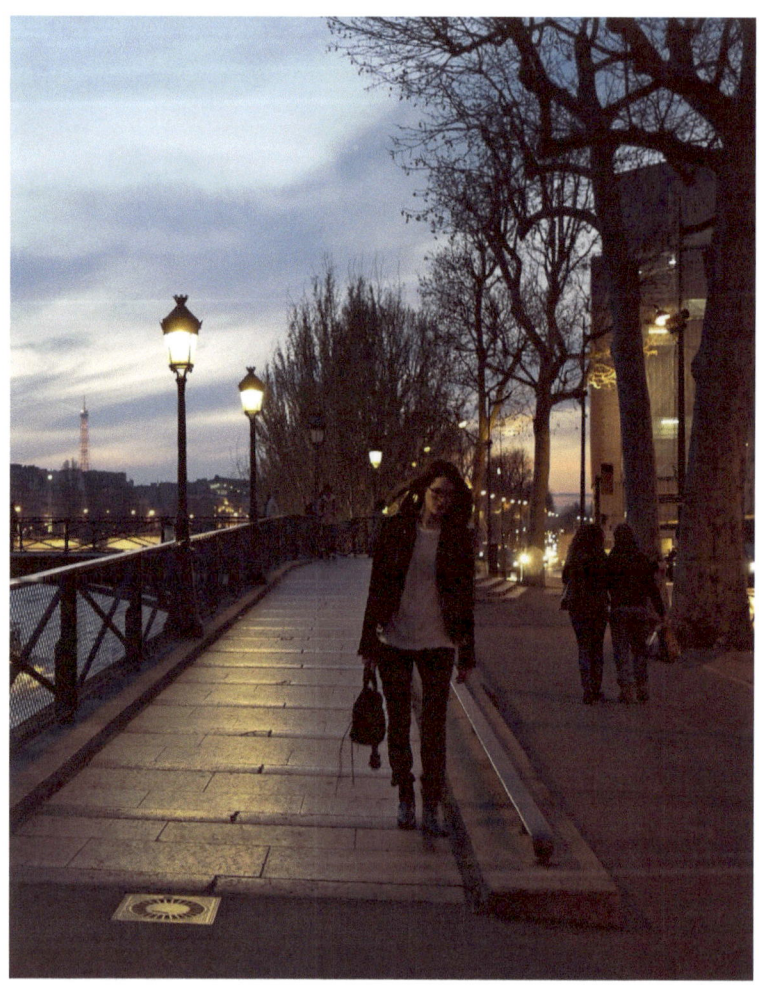

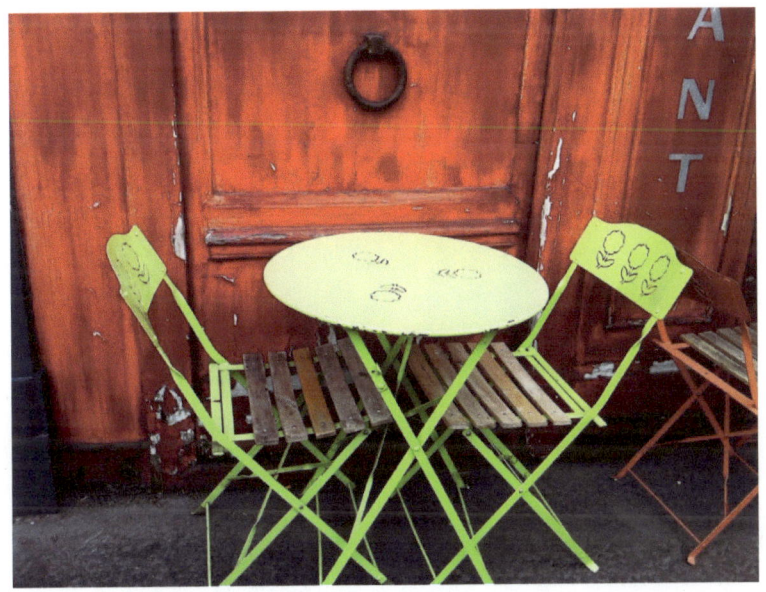

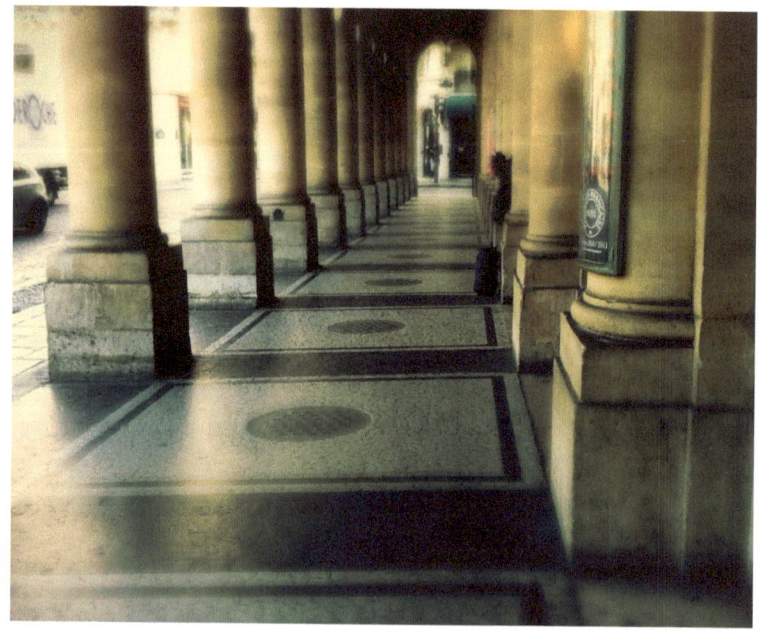

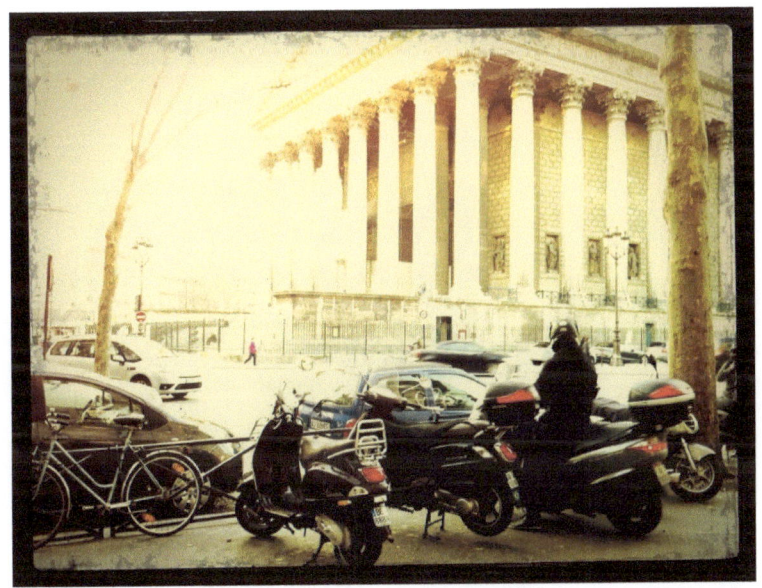

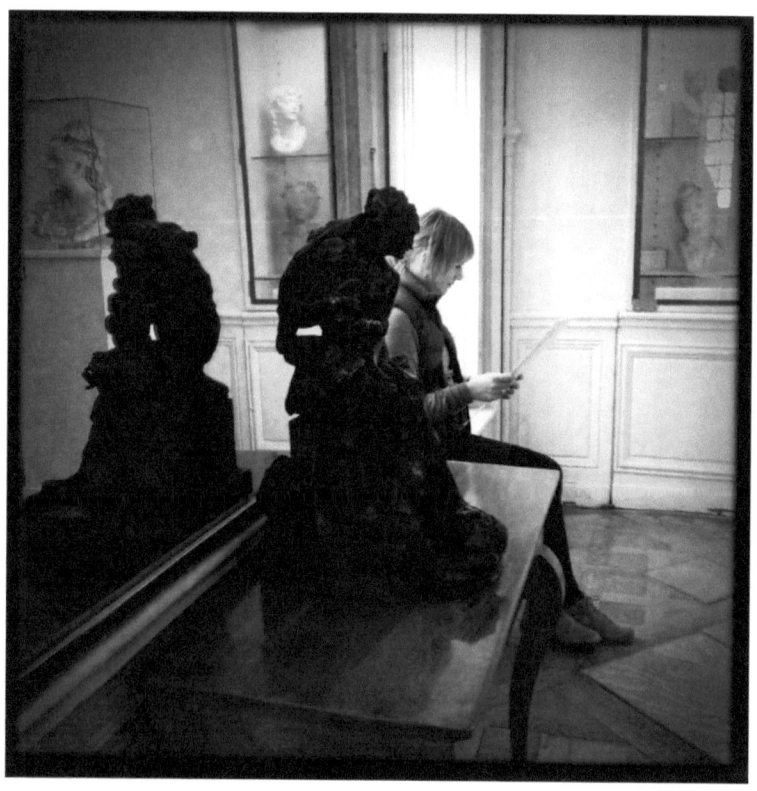

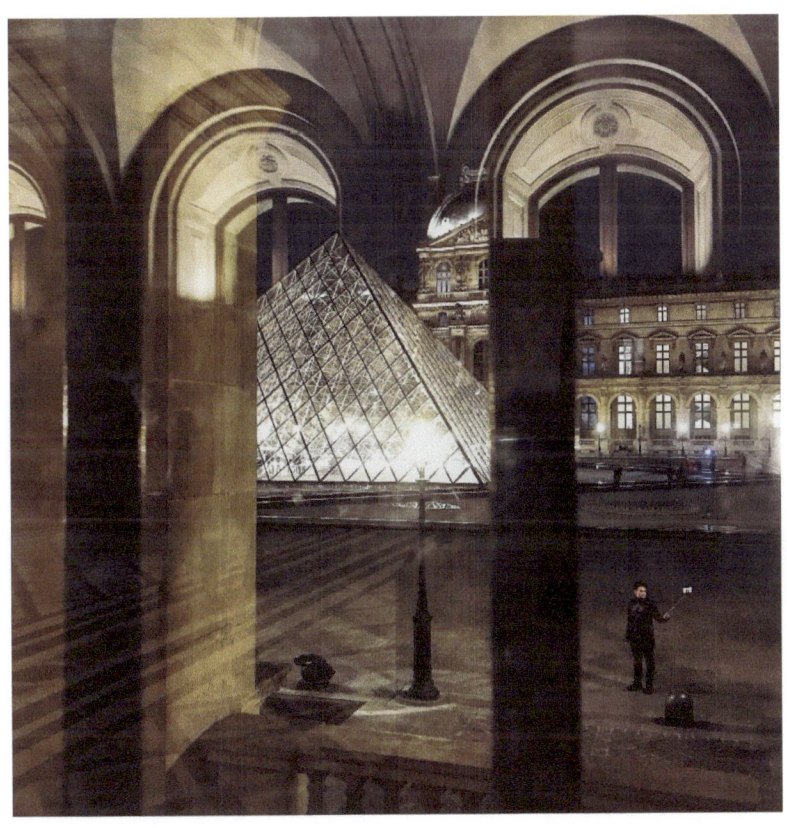

"The last time I saw Paris, her trees were dressed for spring,
And lovers walked beneath those trees and birds found songs to sing."

--Oscar Hammerstein II

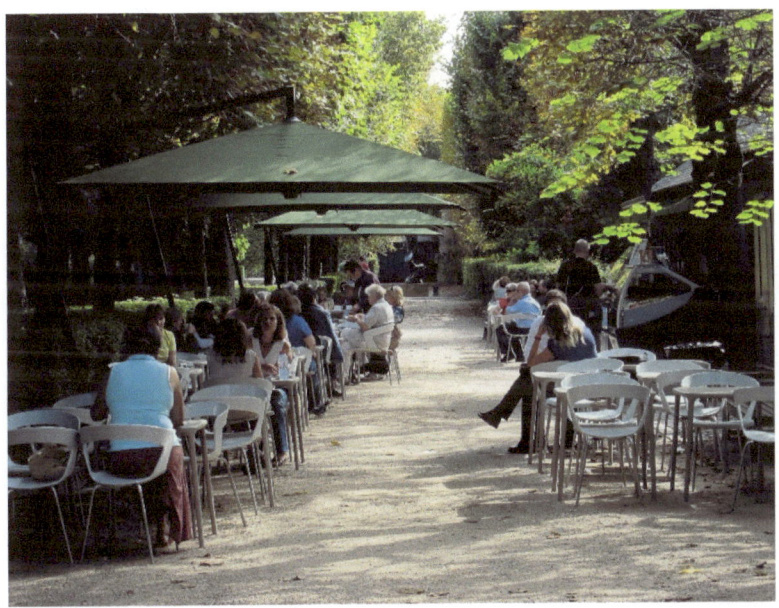

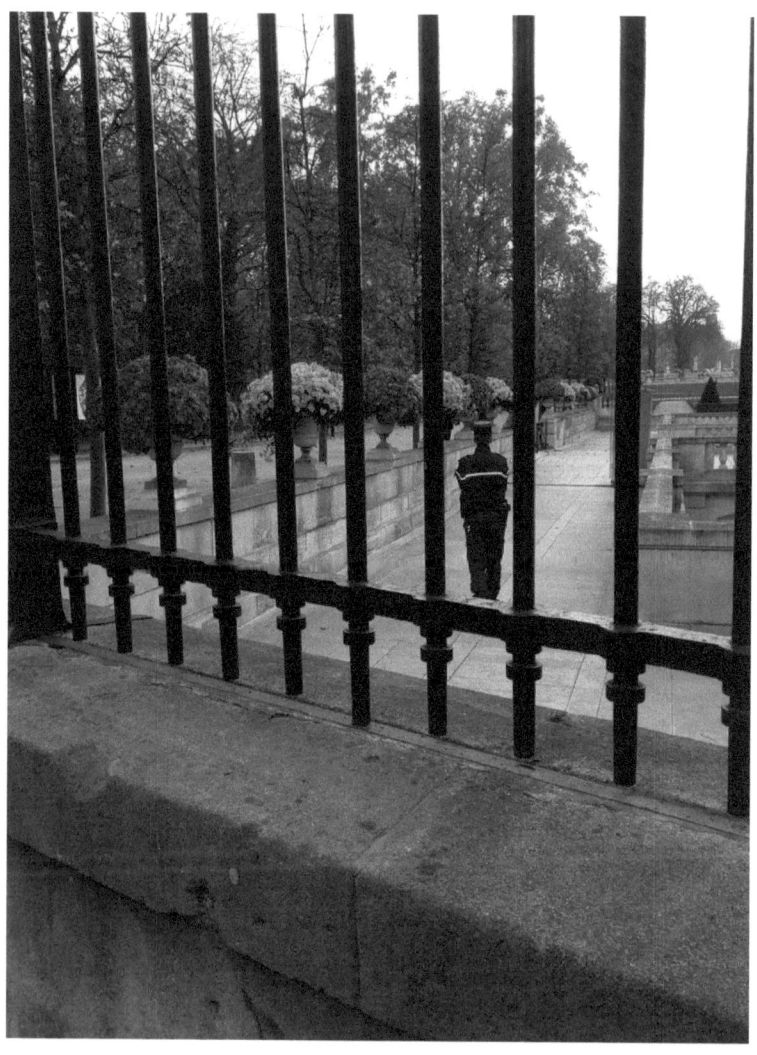

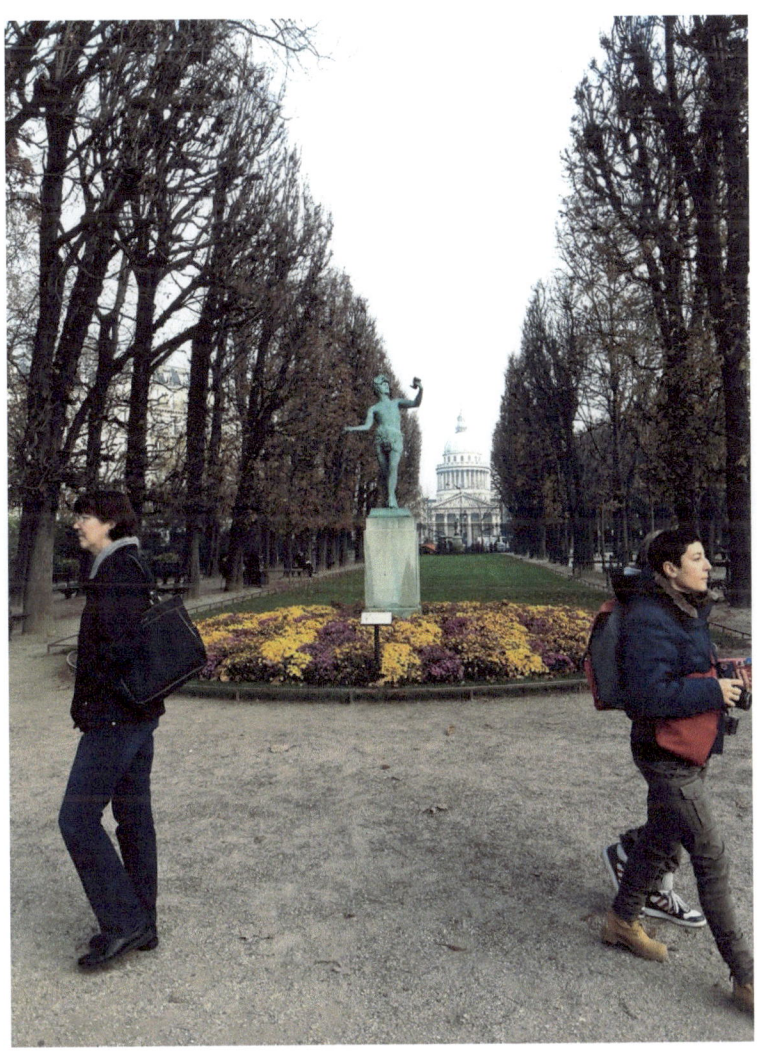

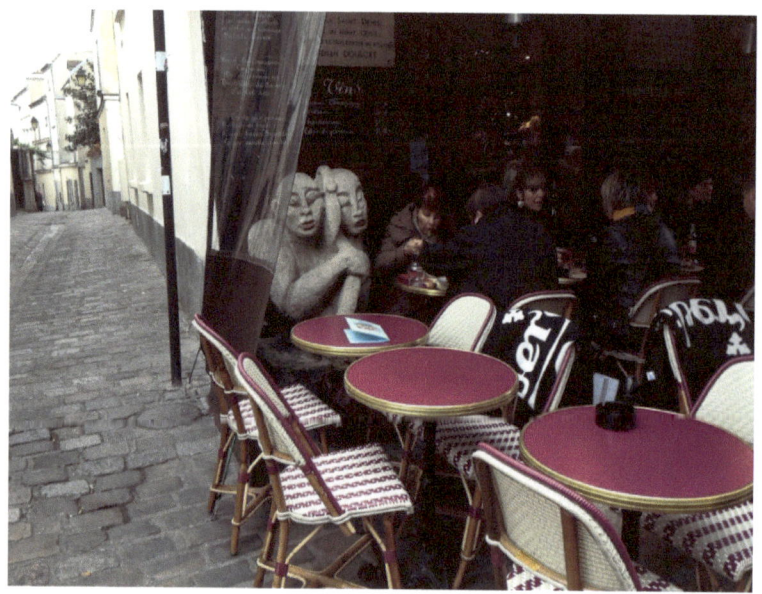

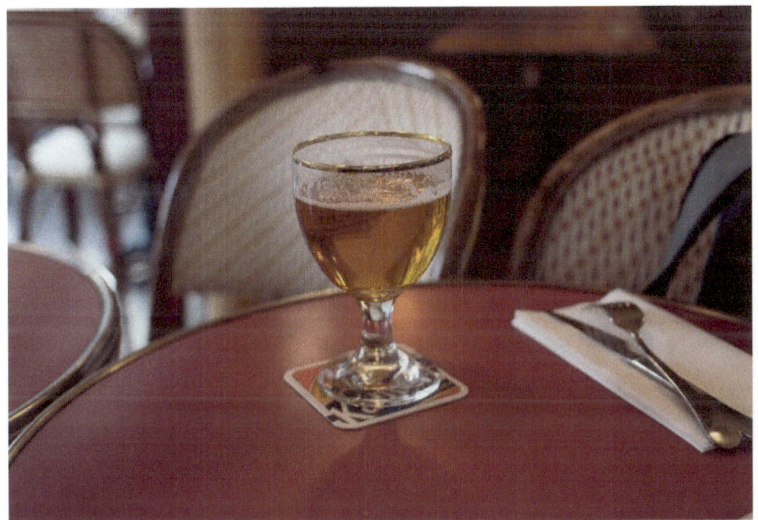

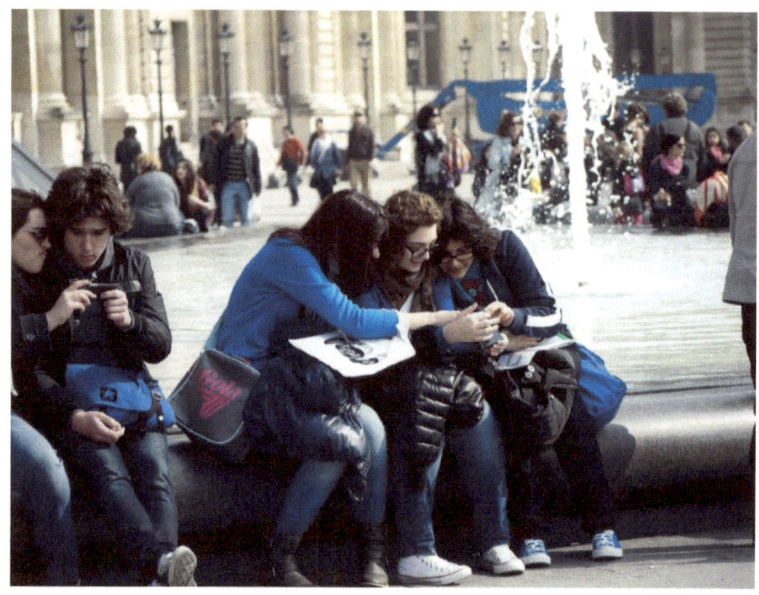

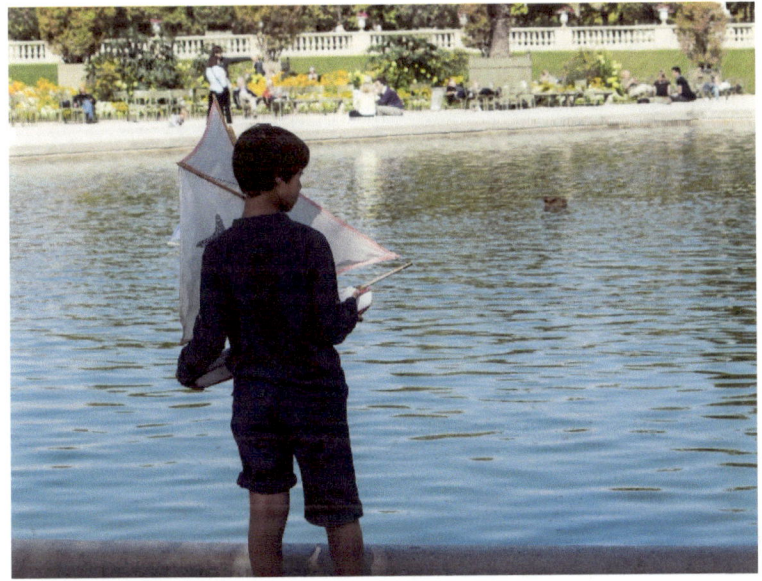

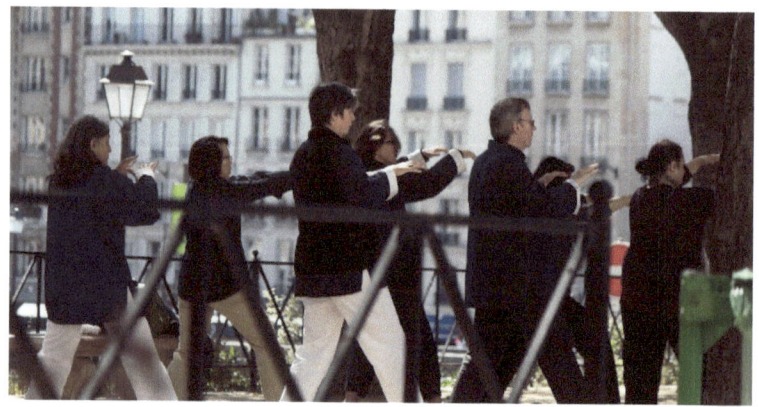

"Born and raised in Paris, I am deeply attached to my city; we almost have half a century of love story together, where I have been truly completely faithful! The most beautiful city in the world is my city, yeepeeee!"

--Christian Louboutin

"I fell in love with pastry because I felt I could be much more creative. It's precise, and you don't have to kill anything."

-- Johnny Iuzzini

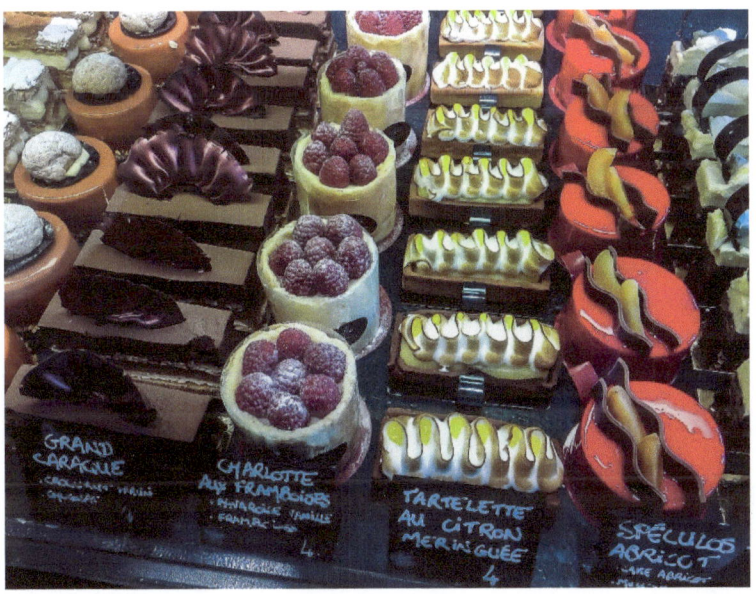

"The best of America drifts to Paris. The American in Paris is the best American. It is more fun for an intelligent person to live in an intelligent country. France has the only two things toward which we drift as we grow older – intelligence and good manners."

--F. Scott Fitzgerald

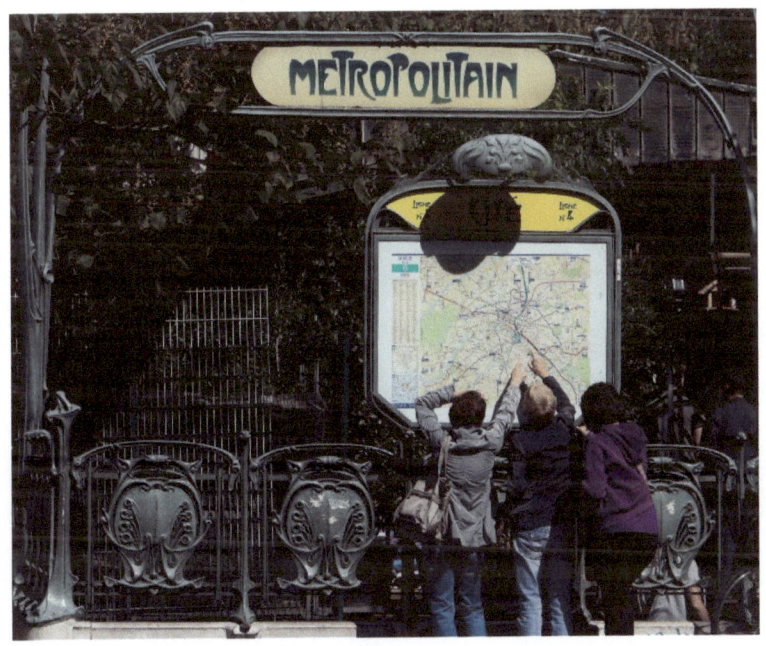

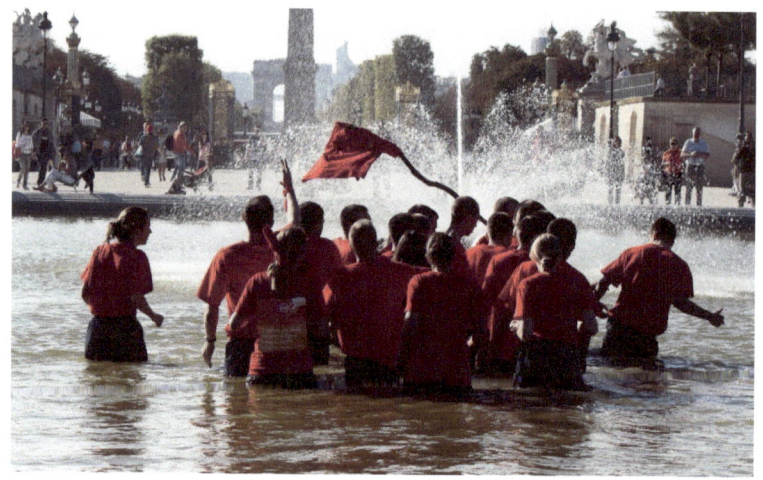

"Paris is a place in which we can forget ourselves, reinvent, expunge the dead weight of our past."

Michael Simkins

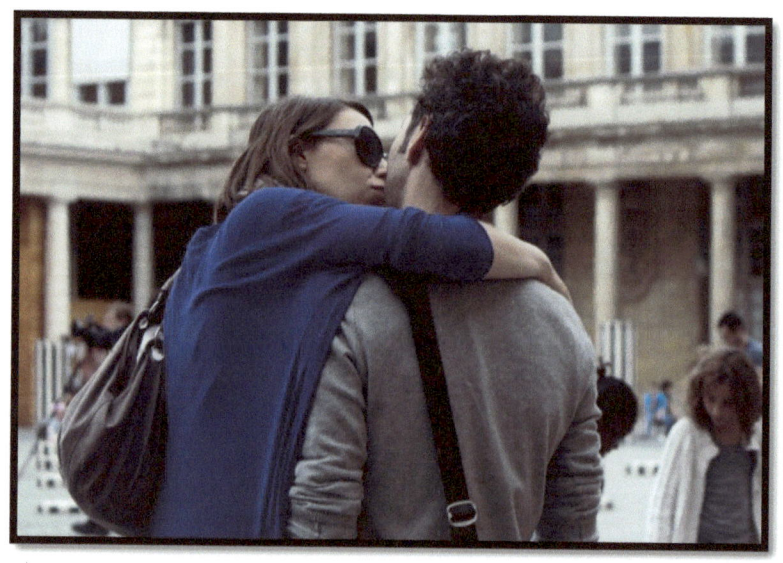

"Our hearts were young and gay."

--Cornelia Otis Skinner

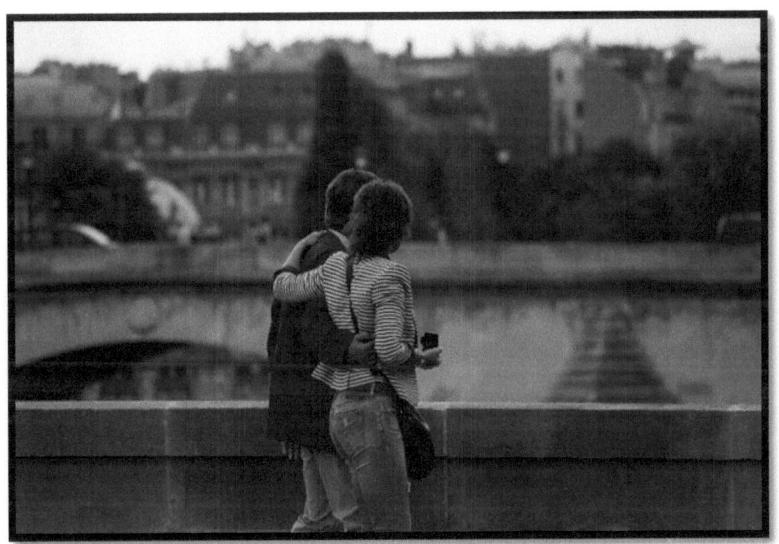

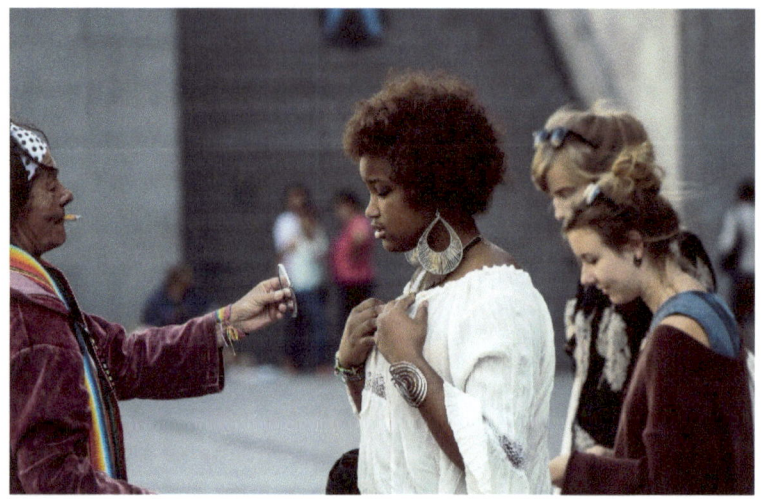

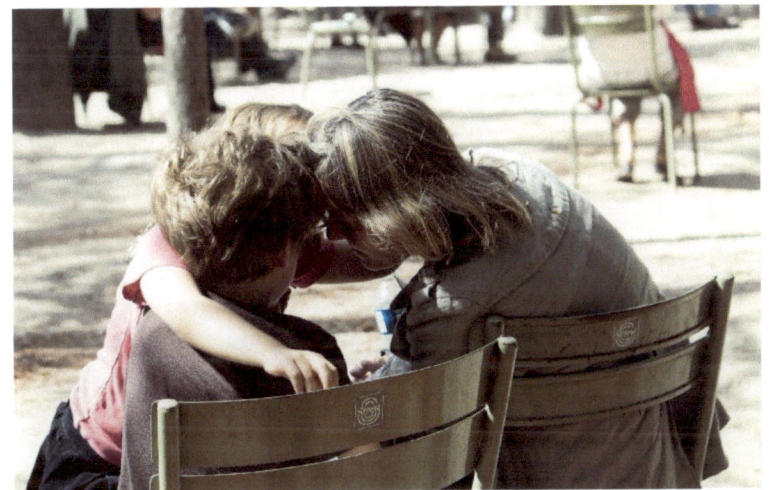

"There may or may not be some truth in this, but in view of the fact that no documentary proof has been obtained that Chaplin was born in the United Kingdom, it may well be that he was in fact born in France."

--Police memo to MI5

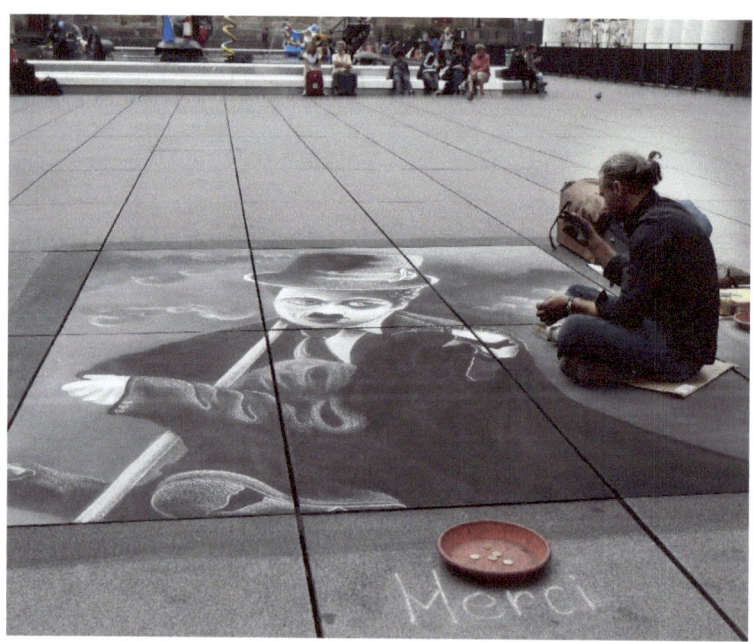

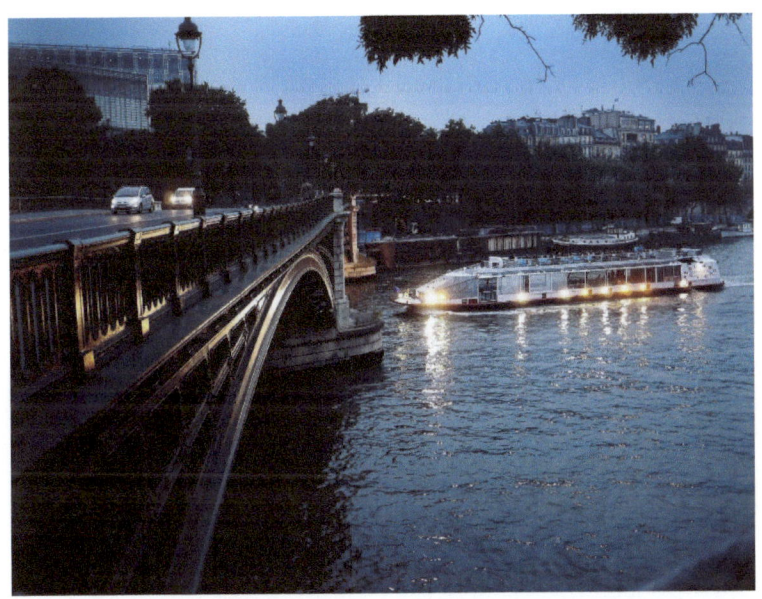

"I can never tire of speaking of the bridges of Paris. By day and by night have I paused on them to gaze at their views; the word not being too comprehensive for the crowds and groupings of objects that are visible from their arches."

-- James Fenimore Cooper

"To err is human. To loaf is Parisian."

--Victor Hugo

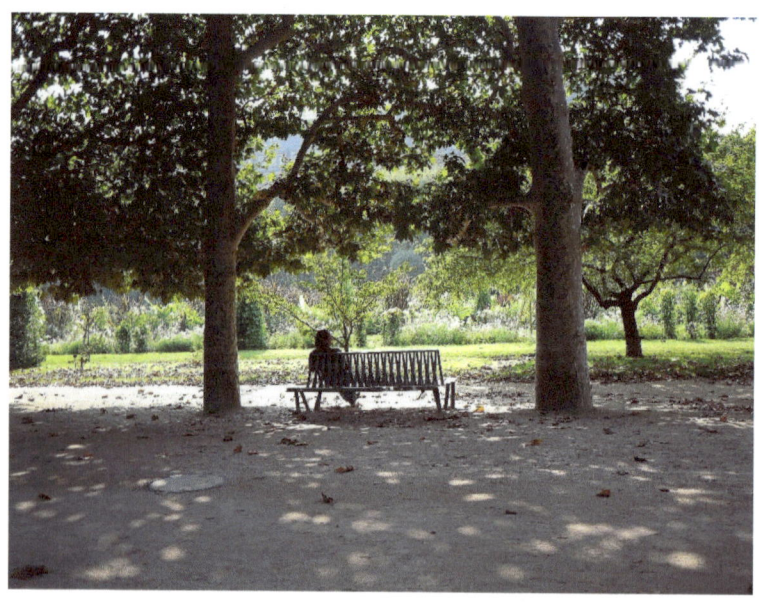

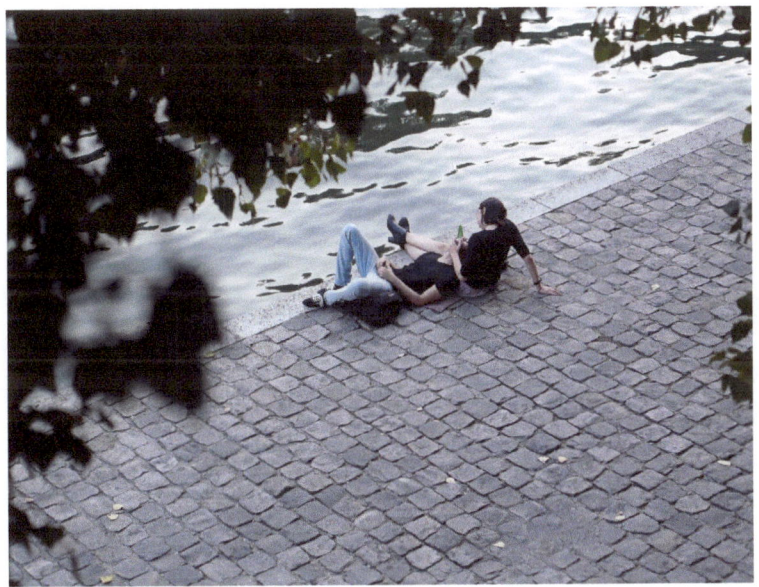

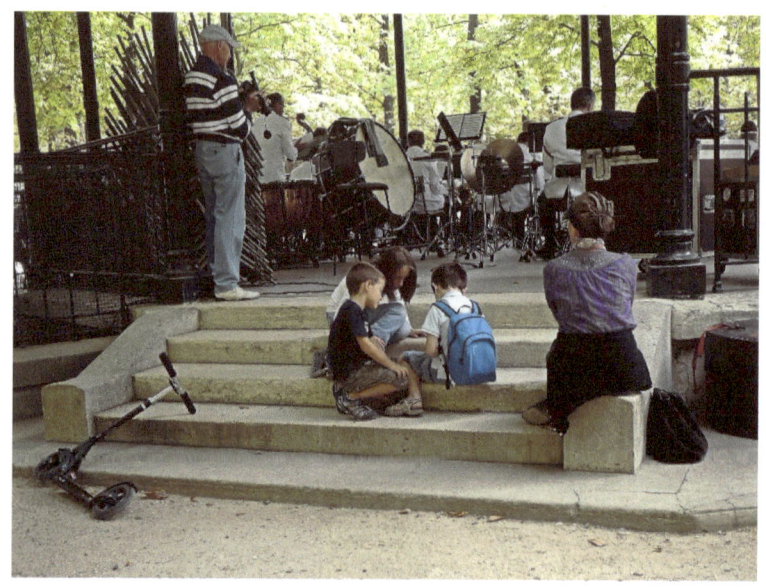

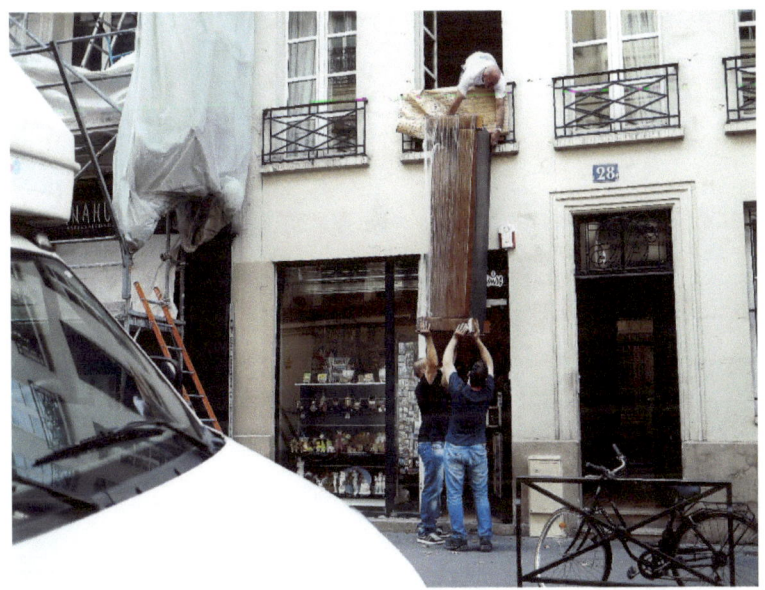

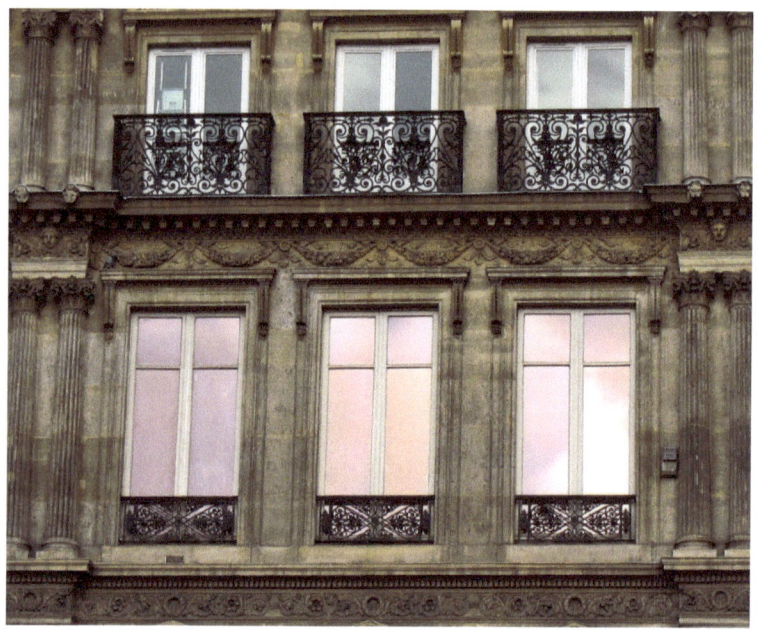

"The passage from the big to the little is what makes Paris beautiful, and you have to be prepared to be small – to live, to trudge, to have your head down in melancholy and to lift it up, sideways – to get it."

--Adam Gopnik

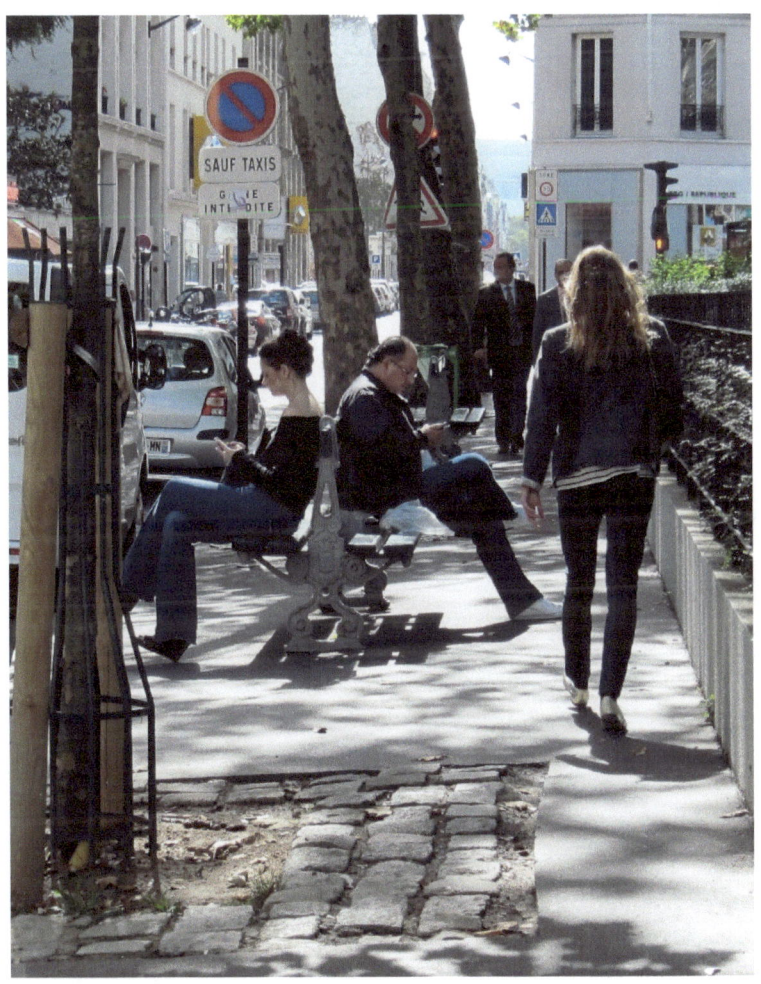

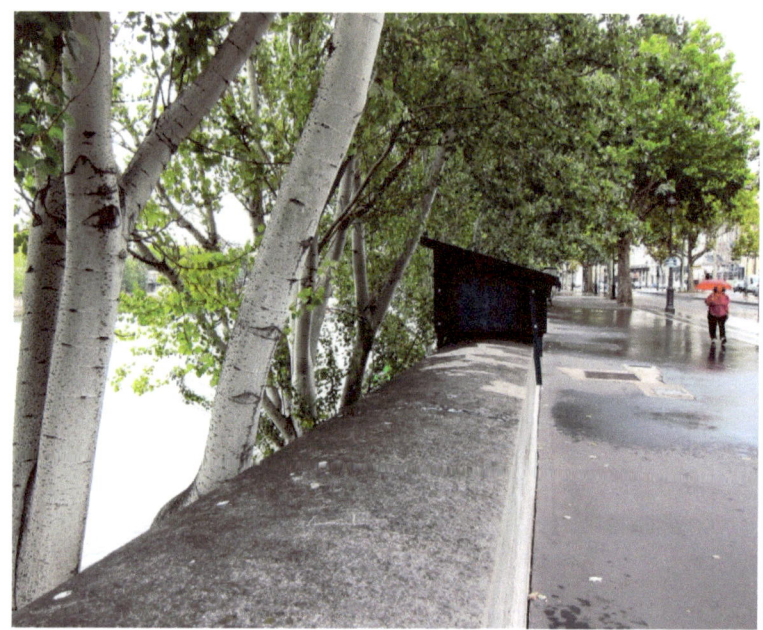

"It's Paris. You don't come here for the weather."

--Adrian Leeds

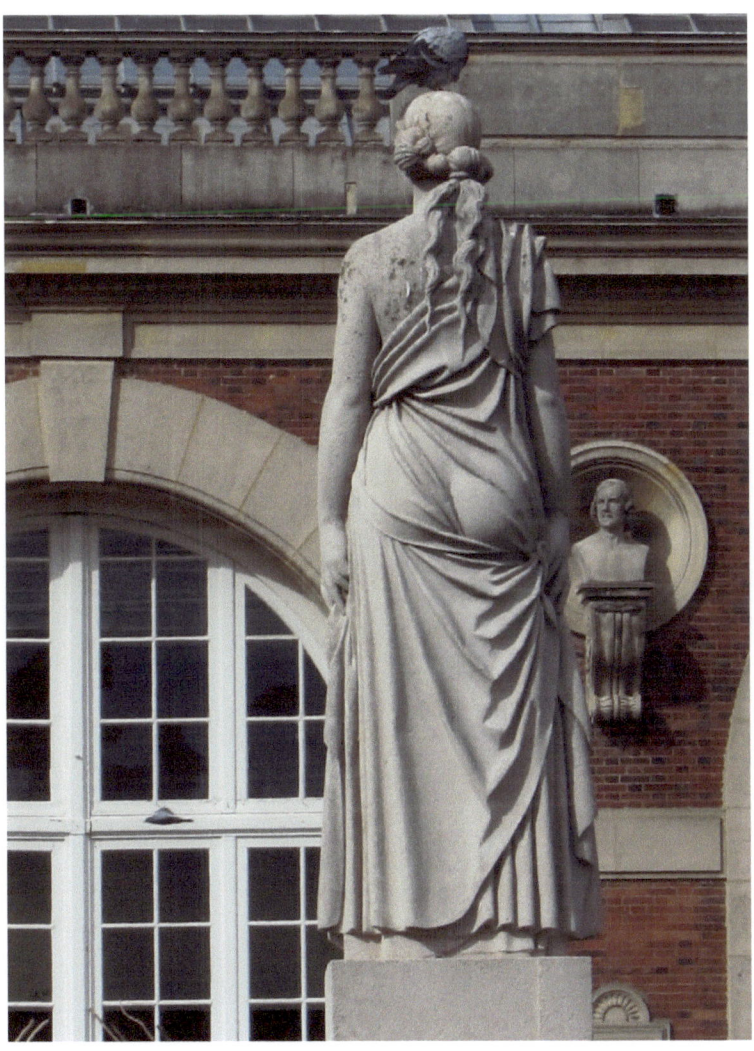

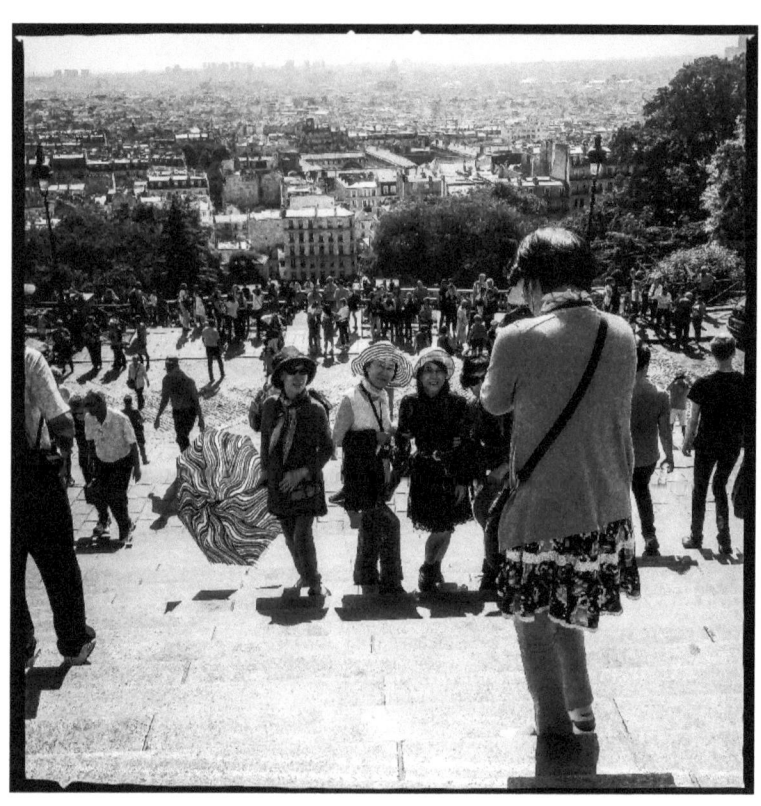

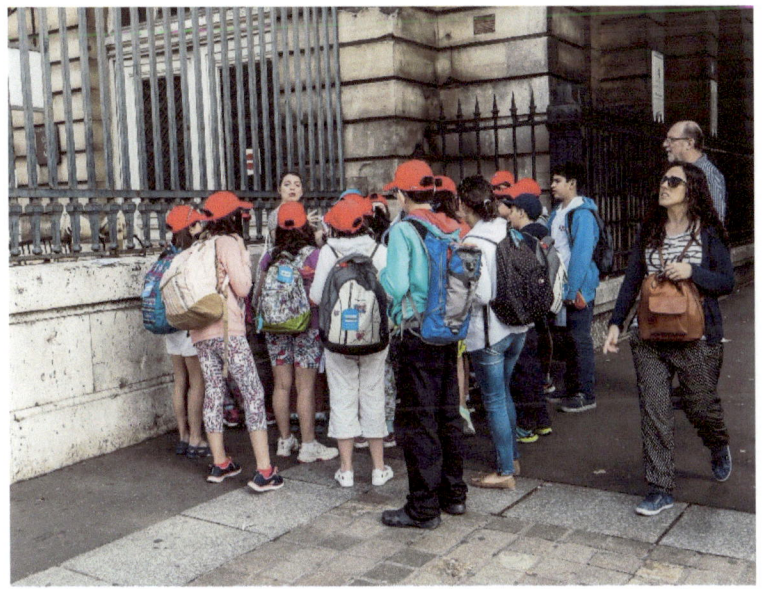

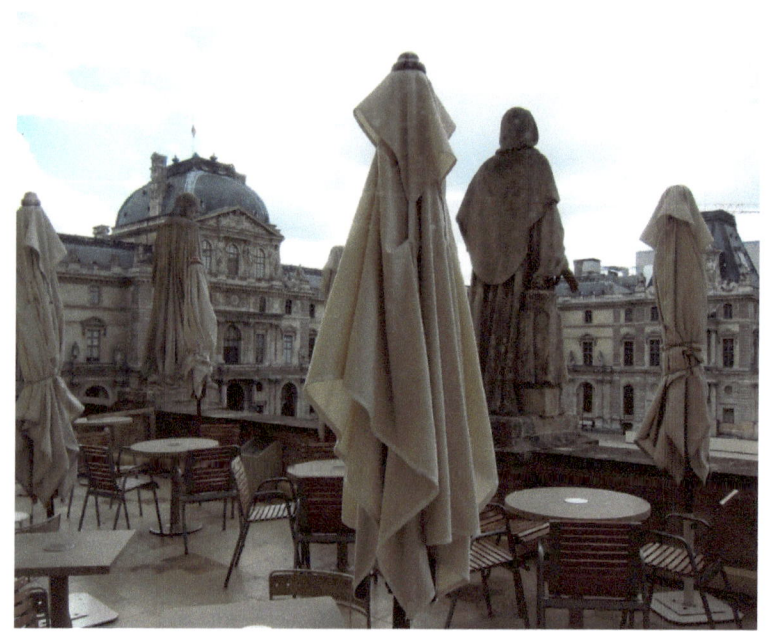

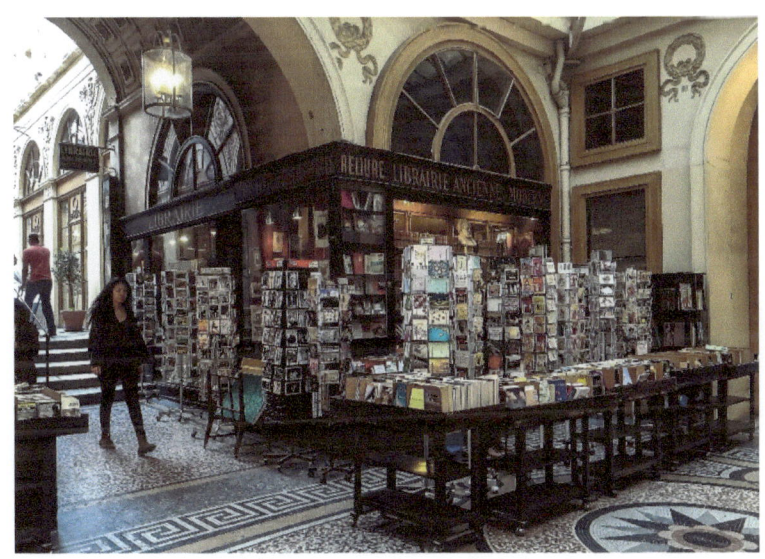

"The Seine, the Seine – When will I again
Meet her there, greet her there
On the moonlit banks of the Seine?"

--Irving Burgess

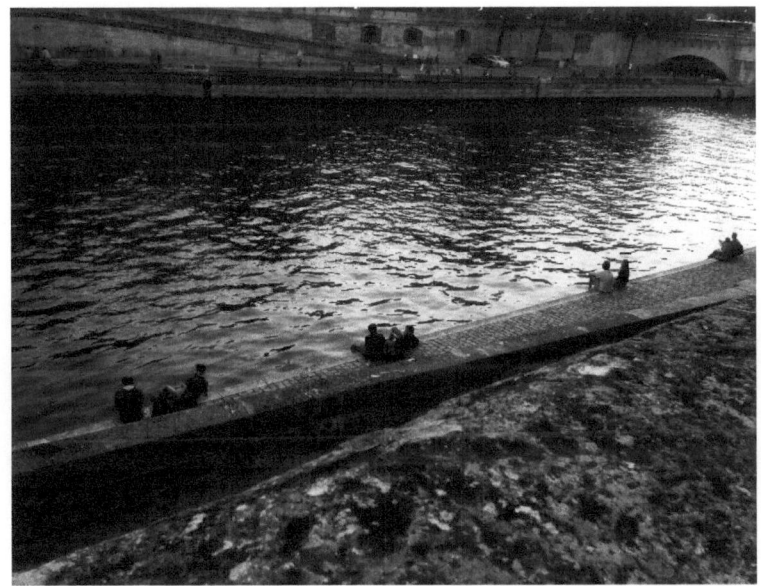

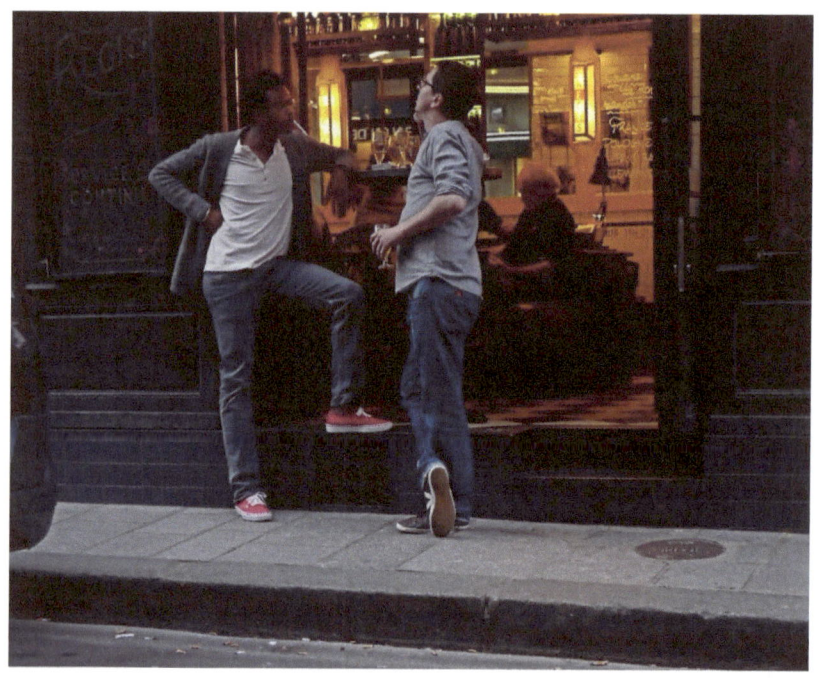

"I like Frenchmen very much, because even when they insult you they do it so nicely."

--Josephine Baker

"When I first went to Paris in 1965, I fell in love with the small, family-owned restaurants that existed everywhere then, as well as the markets and the French obsession with buying fresh food, often twice a day."

--Alice Waters

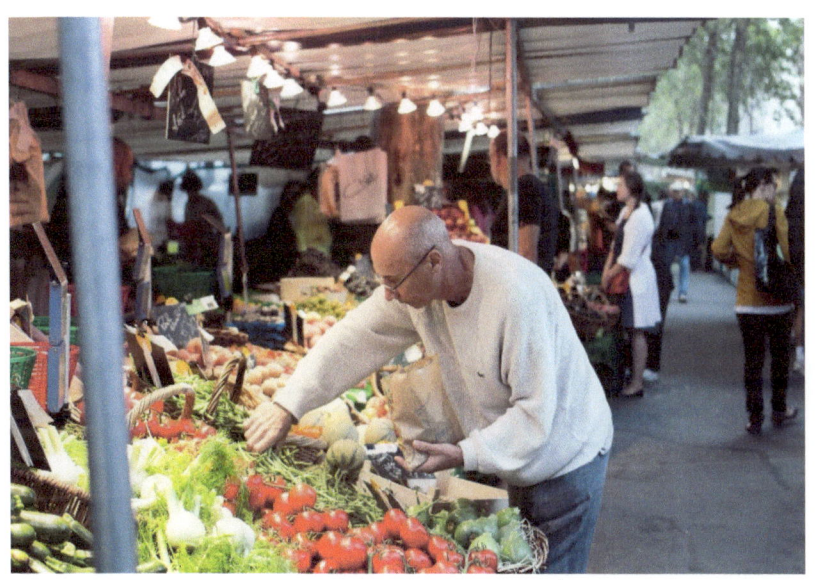

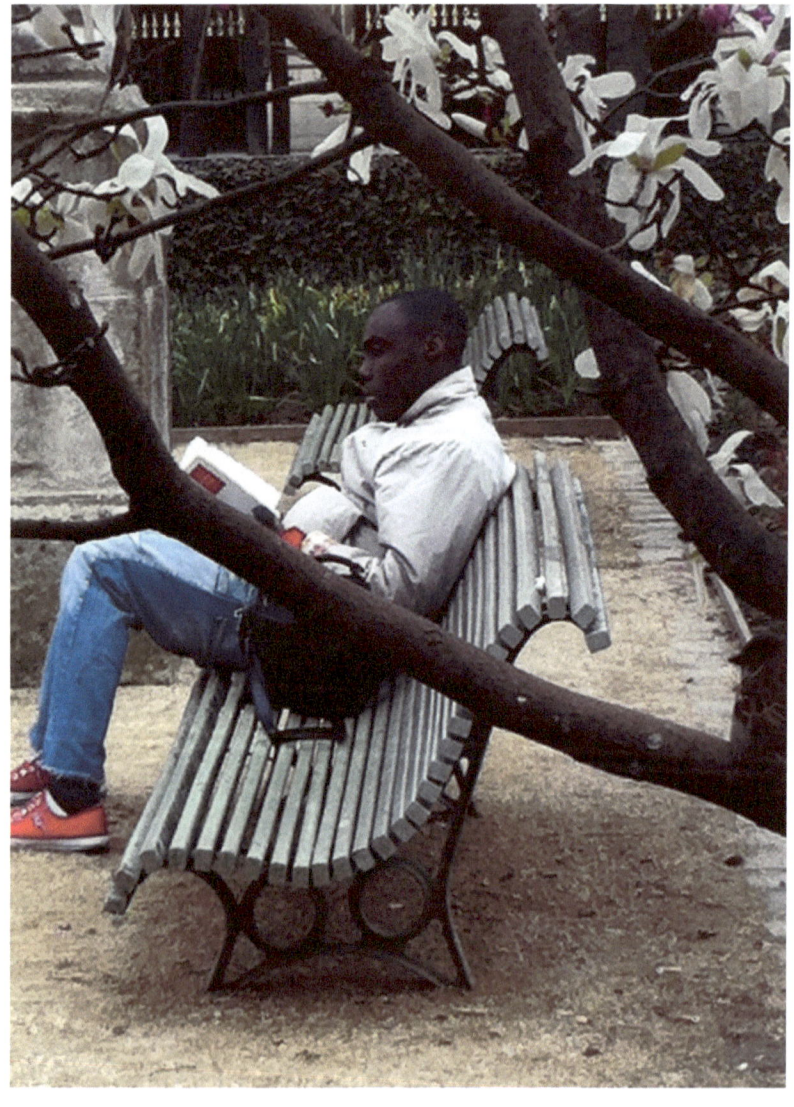

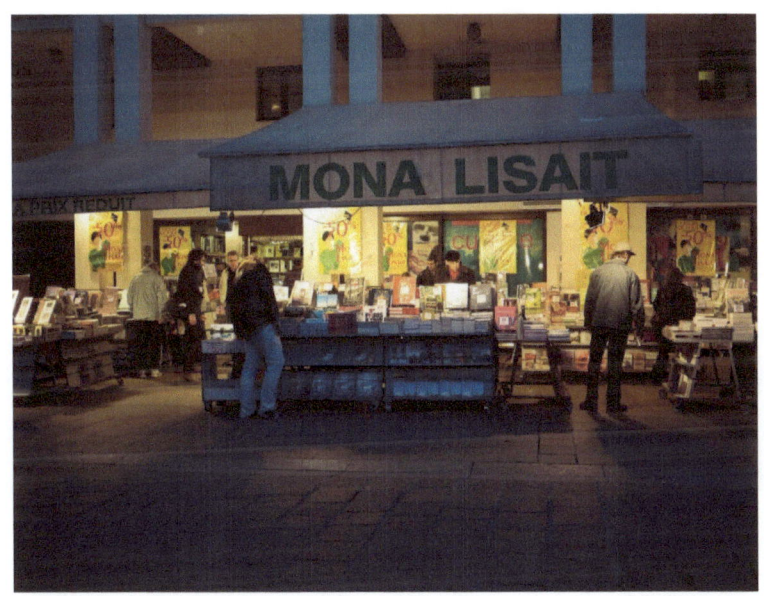

"Writing and reading is to me synonymous with existing."

--Gertrude Stein

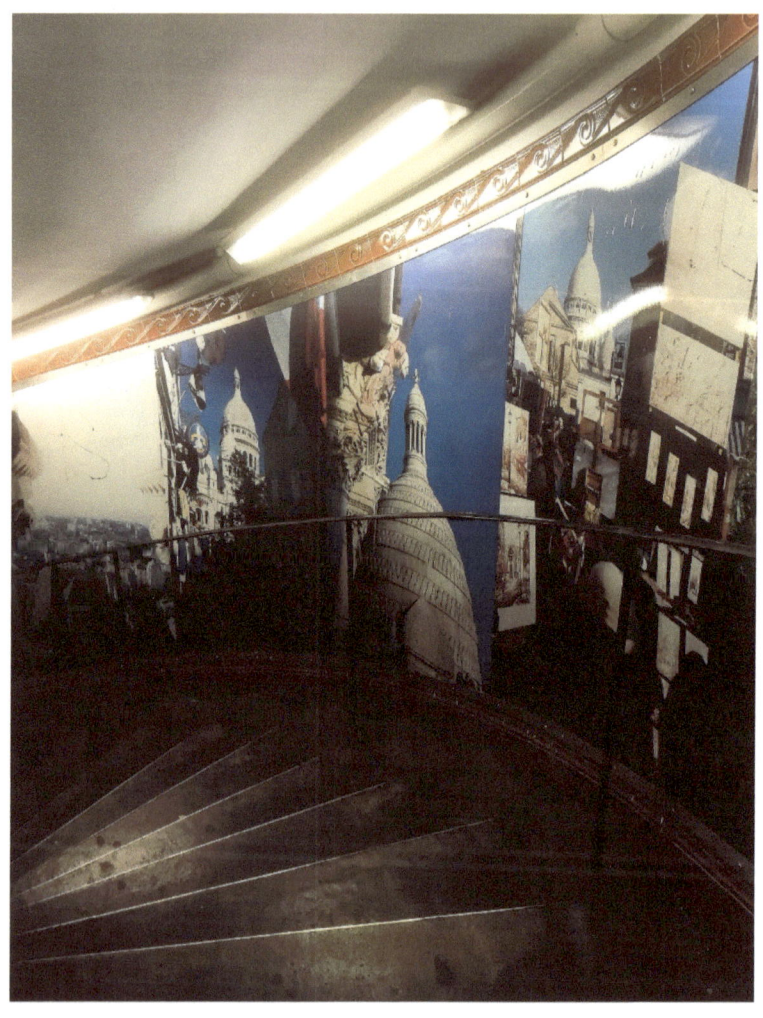

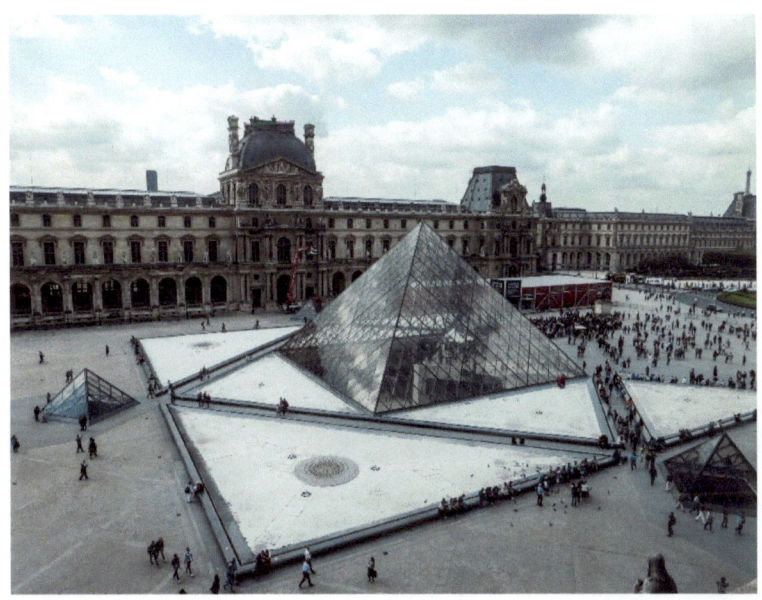

"We had a lot of difficulty in getting the French to accept the pyramid. They thought we were trying to import a piece of Egypt until I pointed out that their obelisk was also from Egypt and the Place des Pyramides is around the corner. Then they accepted it. The pyramid at the Louvre, though, is just the tip."

--I. M. Pei

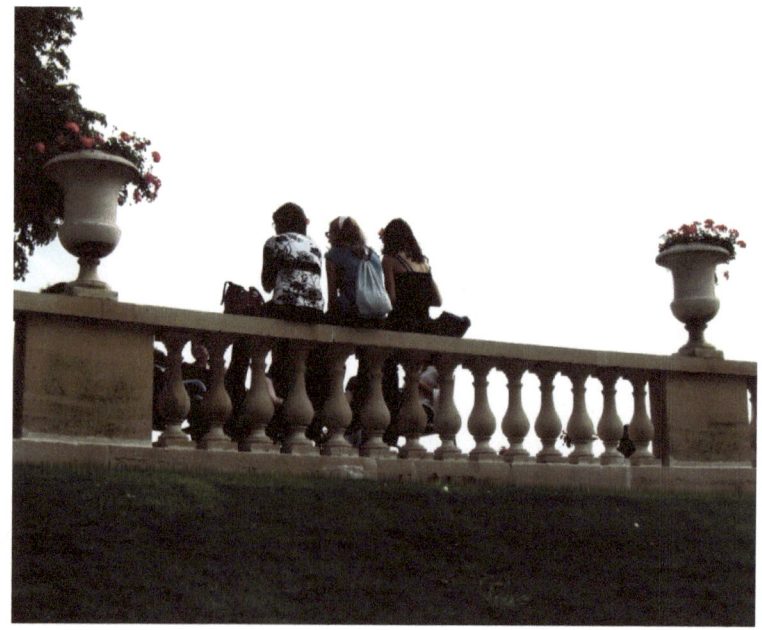

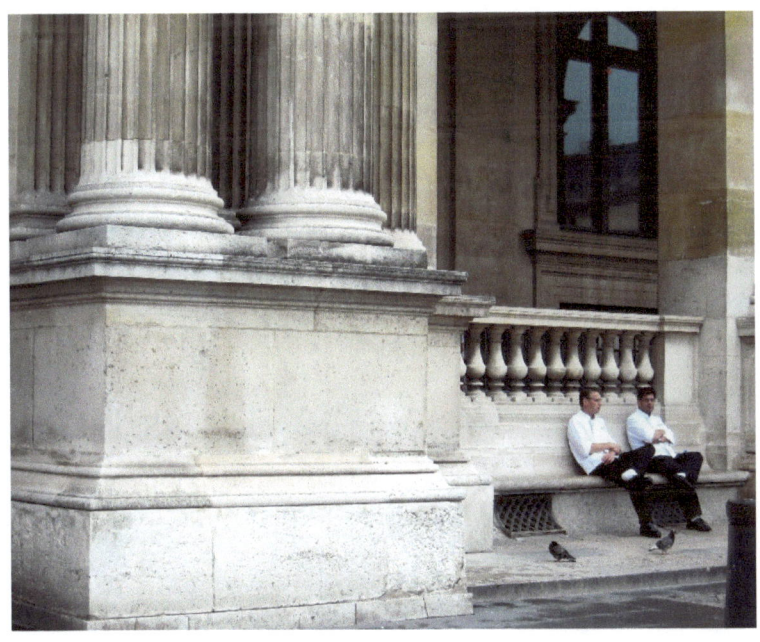

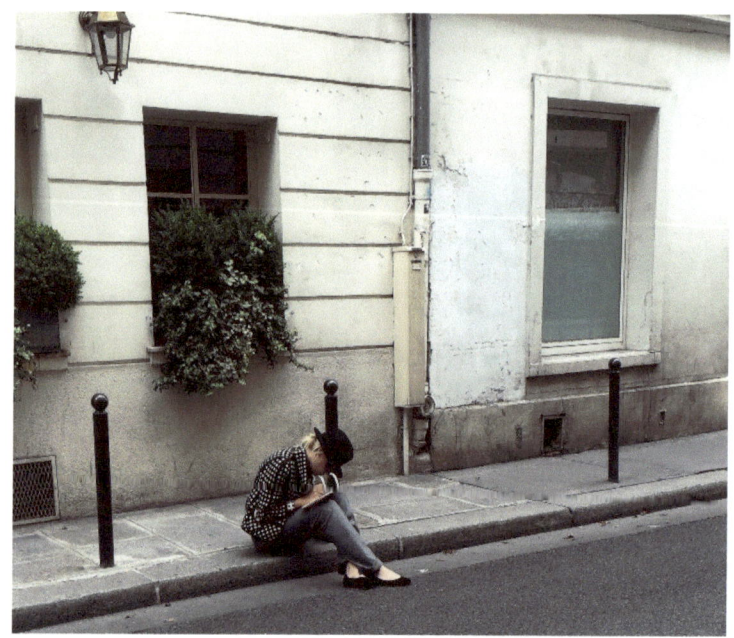

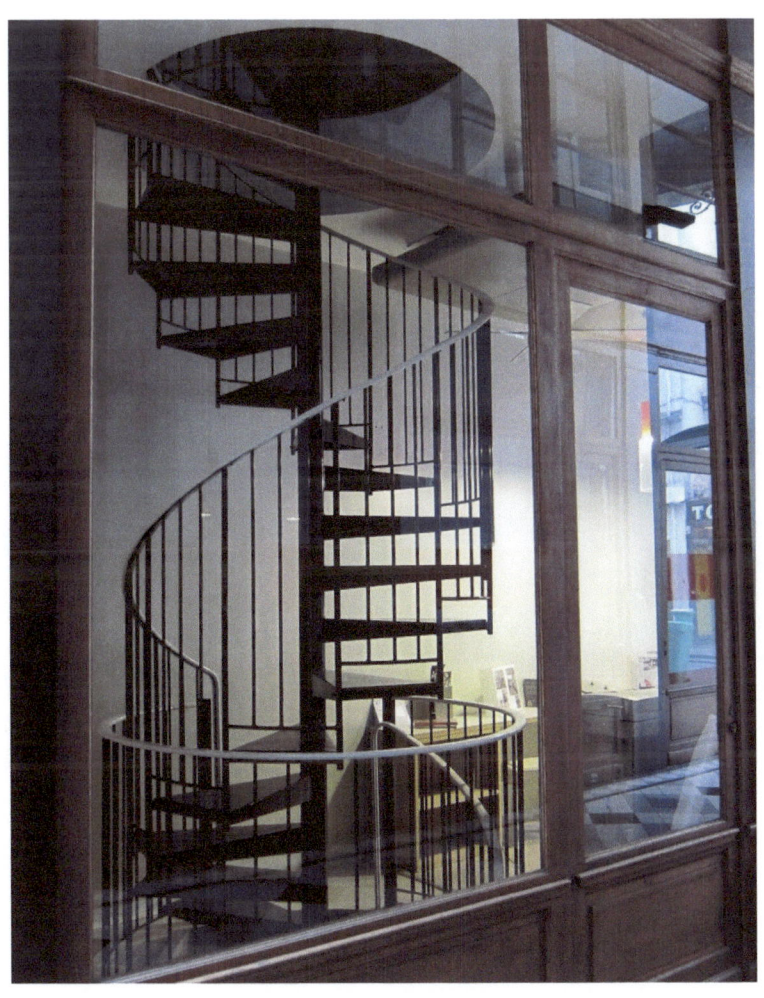

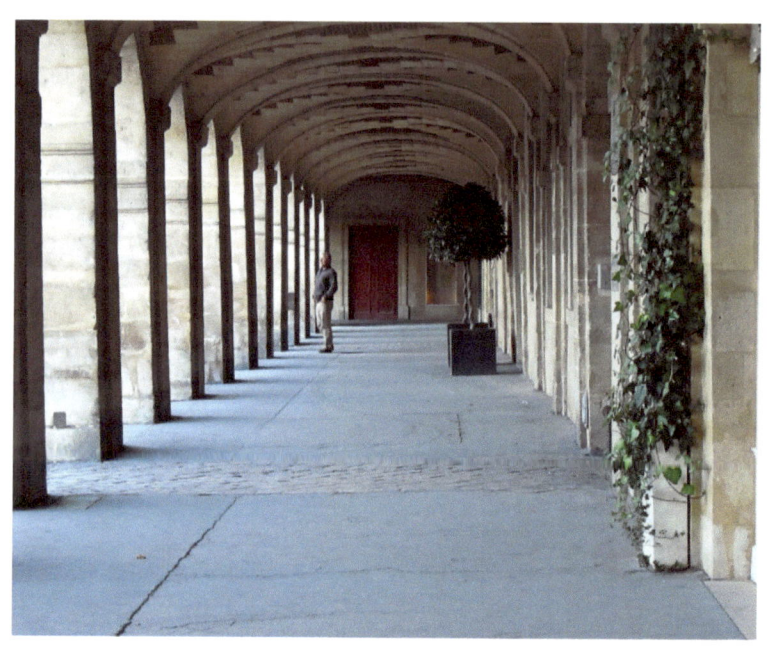

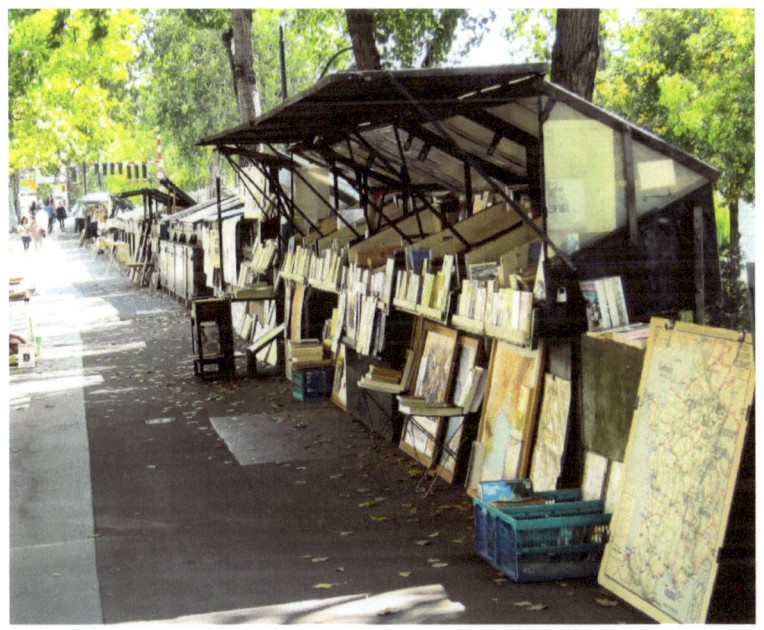

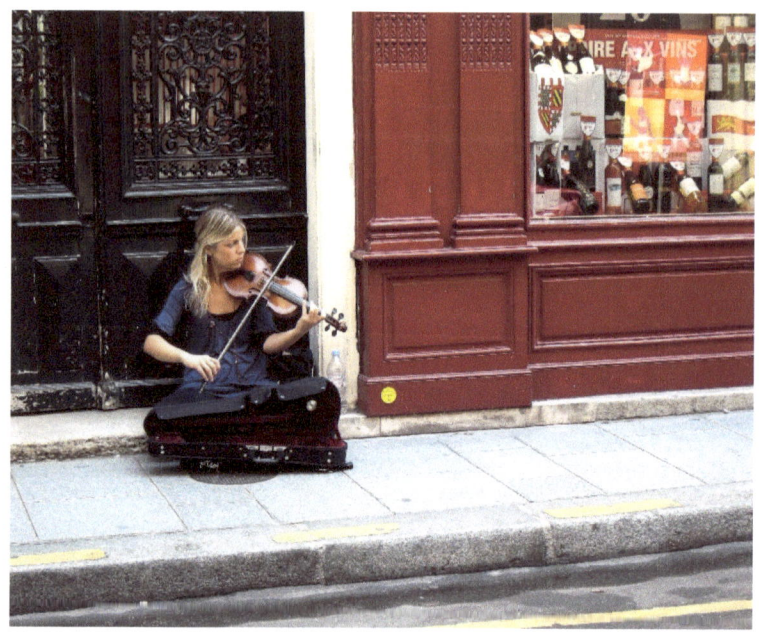

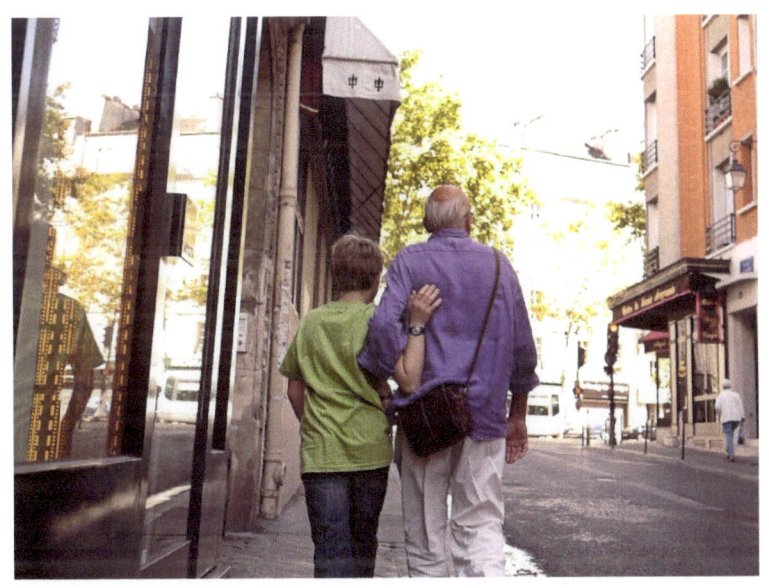

"Paris is an explanation."

--G. K. Chesterton

www.ingramcontent.com/pod-product-compliance
Lightning Source LLC
Chambersburg PA
CBHW040904180526
45159CB00010BA/2917